STUDY NOTES

GATE MECHANICAL

MATERIALS, MANUFACTURING AND INDUSTRIAL ENGINEERING

VOLUME - 3

TABLE OF CONTENT

COMPUTER INTEGRATED MANUFACTURING

COMPUTER INTEGRATED MANUFACTURING (CIM)

Introduction: The meaning and origin of CIM, The changing manufacturing and management scenario, External communication, Islands of automation and software, Dedicated and open systems, Manufacturing automation protocol, Product related activities of a company, Marketing engineering, Production planning, Plant operations, Physical distribution, Business and financial management.

Computer Aided Process planning: Role of process planning in CAD/CAM integration, approaches to computer aided process planning- Variant approach and Generative approaches, CAPP and CMPP process planning systems.

Introduction to CIM

Initially, machine tool automation started with the development of numerical control in 1950s. In less than 50 years, it is amazing that today's manufacturing plants are completely automated. However, establishment of these plants gave relatively a few varieties of product. At first we define what do we mean by a manufacturing plant? Here, we are considering a several categories of manufacturing (or production) for the various manufacturing plants. Manufacturing can be considered in three broad areas:

(i) Continuous process production,
(ii) Mass production, and
(iii) job-shop production.
Among these three, mass production and job-shop production can be categorized as discrete- item production.

Continuous Process Production

Such type of product flows continuously in the manufacturing system, e.g. petroleum, cement, steel rolling, petrochemical and paper production etc. Equipment used here are only applicable for small group of similar products.

Mass Production

It includes the production of discrete unit at very high rate of speed. Discrete item production is used for goods such as automobiles, refrigerators, televisions, electronic component and so on. Mass production contains the character of continuous process production for discrete products. That's why mass production has realized enormous benefits from automation and mechanization.

Job Shop Production

A manufacturing facility that produces a large number of different discrete items and requires different sequences among the production equipments is called job shop. Scheduling and routine problems are the essential features of job shop. As a result, automation has at best been restricted to individual component of job shop. But there have been few attempts in the field of total automation. Physical components of an automated manufacturing system do not include continuous flow process as it only consists of a small percentage of manufacturing system. Mass production of discrete items is included in this category, where segments of production line are largely automated but not the entire line. Job shop facilities have used automated machines, but transfer of work among these machines is a difficult task. Apart from some physical equipment needed, a major component of the automated information that needs to be made available to the manufacturing operation must come from product design. This allows a plant to be automated and integrated. However, manufacturing is more concerned with process design rather than product design.

The characteristic of present world market include higher competition, short product life cycle, greater product diversity, fragmented market, variety and complexity, and smaller batch sizes to satisfy a variety of customer profile. Furthermore, non price factors such as quality of product design innovation and delivery services are the preliminary determinant for the success of product. In today's global arena, to achieve these requirements manufacturing company needs to be flexible, adaptable and responsive to changes and be able to produce a variety of products in short time and at lower cost. These issues attract manufacturing industries to search for some advanced technology, which can overcome these difficulties. Computer integrated manufacturing (CIM), which emerged in 1970, was the outcome of this protracted search.

A CIM System consists of the following basic components:

I. Machine tools and related equipment

II. Material Handling System (MHS)

III. Computer Control System

IV. Human factor/labor

CIM refers to a production system that consists of:

1 A group of NC machines connected together by

2 An automated materials handling system

3 And operating under computer control

In Production Systems CIM is appropriate for batch production as shown in Fig. 1.

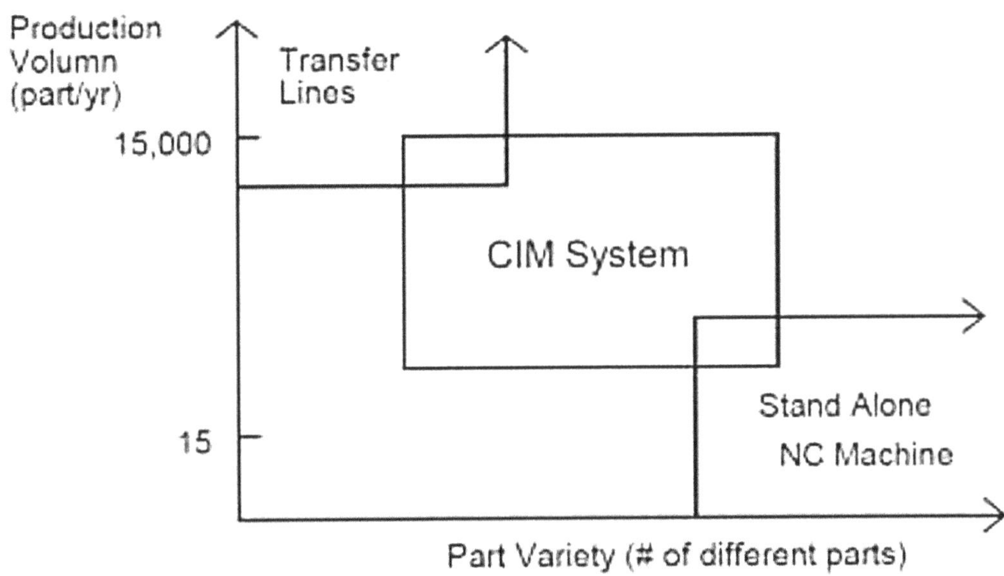

Fig. 1 Application of CIM in Production systems

Transfer Lines: is very efficient when producing "identical" parts in large volumes at high product rates.

Stand Alone: NC machine: are ideally suited for variations in work part configuration. CIM involves a fundamental strategy of integrating manufacturing facilities and systems in an enterprise through the computer and it's peripheral. CIM can be defined in different ways depending upon its application. CIM involves integration of advanced technologies in various functional units of an enterprise, in an effective manner to achieve the success of the manufacturing industries. A deep knowledge and understanding of all the technology is required for an effective integration. At first integration of advanced manufacturing technology (AMT) is required to get success in the application of CIM. Computers act as a subordinate to the technologies. Computers help, organize, and restore information in order to achieve high accuracy and speed. Their basic aim is to achieve the goals of the objectives within limited available capital. Traditionally, all the efforts were focused on achieving single goal to improve the effectiveness and competitiveness of the organization. But they failed because they didn't satisfy the overall objectives of the manufacturing companies. Hence, a multiple goal selection or mult- criteria optimization is proposed to make the CIM an effective tool to improve the economy of the company. The new approach should be developed for improving the existing multi-criteria optimization mechanism, so that CIM can be realized globally. In addition, global integration approach should be applied to make globally distributed company as a single entity. This concept is applied to make virtual CIM more effective and hence helps in meeting the present global economic circumstances using intelligent manufacturing. Therefore, manufacturing technology should be blended with intelligence. This will help manufacturing enterprise to produce better quality. It will also facilitate the manufacturing equipments to solve problems posed during normal course of the operations.

Computer technology is the necessary input to implement automation in manufacturing system. The term CIM denotes the widespread use of computer systems to design the product, to plan the production, control the operation, and perform the business related functions required in the manufacturing firm. True CIM includes integration of these functions in the system that operates throughout the enterprise. Other words are used to identify specific element of the CIM system. For example, computer aided design (CAD) denotes the use of computer system to support the product design system. Computer aided manufacturing (CAM) denotes the use of computer system to perform the functions related to manufacturing engineering, such as process planning and numerically controlled (NC) part programming. Some computer system performs the CAD and CAM, and so the term CAD/CAM is used to indicate the integration of the two systems into one. In addition to CAD/CAM, CIM also includes the firm business function that is related to manufacturing.

Computer Integrated Manufacturing (CIM) encompasses the entire range of productdevelopment and manufacturing activities with all the functions being carried out with the help of dedicated software packages. The data required for various functions are passed from one application software to another in a seamless manner. For example, the product data is created during design. This data has to be transferred from the modeling software to manufacturing software without any loss of data. CIM uses a common database wherever feasible and communication technologies to integrate design, manufacturing and associated business functions that combine the automated segments of a factory or a manufacturing facility. CIM reduces the human component of manufacturing and thereby relieves the process of its slow, expensive and error-prone component. CIM stands for a holistic and methodological approach to the activities of the manufacturing enterprise in order to achieve vast improvement in its performance. This methodological approach is applied to all activities from the design of the product tocustomer support in an integrated way, using various methods, means and techniques inorder to achieve production improvement, cost reduction, fulfillment of scheduled delivery dates, quality improvement and total flexibility in the manufacturing system. CIM requires all those associated with a company to involve totally in the process of product development and manufacture. In such a holistic approach, economic, social and human aspects have the same importance as technical aspects. CIM also encompasses the whole lot of enabling technologies including total quality management, business process reengineering, concurrent engineering, workflow automation, enterprise resource planning and flexible manufacturing.

Manufacturing industries strive to reduce the cost of the product continuously to remain competitivein the face of global competition. In addition, there is the need to improve the quality and performance levels on a continuing basis. Another important requirement is on time delivery. In the context of global outsourcing and long supply chains cutting across several international borders, the task of continuously reducing delivery times is really an arduous task. CIM has several software tools to address the above needs.

Manufacturing engineers are required to achieve the following objectives to be competitive in a global context.

- Reduction in inventory
- Lower the cost of the product.
- Reduce waste
- Improve quality
- Increase flexibility in manufacturing to achieve immediate and rapid response to:
- Product changes
- Production changes
- Process change
- Equipment change
- Change of personnel

CIM technology is an enabling technology to meet the above challenges to the manufacturing.

Evolution of Computer Integrated Manufacturing

Computer Integrated Manufacturing (CIM) is considered a natural evolution of thetechnology of CAD/CAM which by itself evolved by the integration of CAD and CAM. Massachusetts Institute of Technology (MIT, USA) is credited with pioneering the development in both CAD and CAM. The need to meet the design and manufacturing requirements of aerospace industries after the Second World War necessitated the development these technologies. The manufacturing technology available during late 40's and early 50's could not meet the design and manufacturing challenges arising out of the need to develop sophisticated aircraft and satellite launch vehicles. This prompted the US Air Force to approach MIT to develop suitable control systems, drives and programming techniques for machine tools using electronic control.

The first major innovation in machine control is the Numerical Control (NC), demonstrated at MIT in 1952. Early Numerical Control Systems were all basically hardwired systems, since these were built with discrete systems or with later first-generation integrated chips. Early NC machines used paper tape as an input medium. Every NC machine was fitted with a tape reader to read paper tape and transfer the program to the memory of the machine tool block by block. Mainframe computers were used to control a group of NC machines by mid 60's. This arrangement was then called Direct Numerical Control (DNC) as the computer bypassed the tape reader to transfer the program data to the machine controller. By late 60 's minicomputers were being commonly used to control NC machines. At this stage NC became truly soft wired with the facilities of mass program storage, offline editing and software logic control and processing. This development is called Computer Numerical Control (CNC). Since 70's, numerical controllers are being designed around microprocessors, resulting in compact CNC systems. A further development to this technology is the distributed numerical control (also called DNC) in which processing of NC program is carried out in different computers operating at different hierarchical levels - typically from mainframe host computers to plant computers to the machine controller. Today the CNC systems are built around powerful 32 bit and 64 bit microprocessors. PC based systems are also becoming increasingly popular. Manufacturing engineers also started using computers for such tasks like inventory control; demand forecasting, production planning and control etc. CNC technology was adapted in the development of co-ordinate measuring machine's (CMMs) which automated inspection. Robots were introduced to automate several tasks like machine loading, materials handling, welding, painting and assembly. All these developments led to the evolution of flexible manufacturing cells and flexible manufacturing systems in late 70 's.

Evolution of Computer Aided Design (CAD), on the other hand was to cater to the geometric modeling needs of automobile and aeronautical industries. The developments in computers, design workstations, graphic cards, display devices and graphic input and output devices during the last ten years have been phenomenal. This coupled with the development of operating system with graphic user interfaces and powerful interactive (user friendly) software packages for modeling, drafting, analysis and optimization provides the necessary tools to automate the design process.

CAD in fact owes its development to the APT language project at MIT in early 50's. Several clones of APT were introduced in 80's to automatically develop NC codes from the geometric model of the component. Now, one can model, draft, analyze, simulate, modify, optimize and create the NC code to manufacture a component and simulate the machining operation sitting at a computer workstation. If we review the manufacturing scenario during 80's we will find that the manufacturing is characterized by a few islands of automation. In the case of design, the task is well automated. In the case of manufacture, CNC machines, DNC systems, FMC, FMS etc provide tightly controlled automation systems. Similarly computer control has been implemented in several areas like manufacturing resource planning, accounting, sales, marketing and purchase. Yet the full potential of computerization could not be obtained unless all the segments of manufacturing are integrated, permitting the transfer of data across various functional modules. This realization led to the concept of computer integrated manufacturing. Thus the implementation of CIM required the development of whole lot of computer technologies related to hardware and software.

CIM Hardware and CIM Software

CIM Hardware comprises the following:

i. Manufacturing equipment such as CNC machines or computerized work centers, robotic work cells, DNC/FMS systems, work handling and tool handling devices, storage devices, sensors, shop floor data collection devices, inspection machines etc.

ii. Computers, controllers, CAD/CAM systems, workstations / terminals, data entry terminals, bar code readers, RFID tags, printers, plotters and other peripheral devices, modems, cables, connectors etc., CIM software comprises computer programmes to carry out the following functions:

- Management Information System
- Sales
- Marketing
- Finance
- Database Management
- Modeling and Design
- Analysis
- Simulation
- Communications
- Monitoring
- Production Control
- Manufacturing Area Control
- Job Tracking
- Inventory Control
- Shop Floor Data Collection
- Order Entry
- Materials Handling
- Device Drivers - Process Planning
- Manufacturing Facilities Planning
- Workflow Automation
- Business Process Engineering
- Network Management
- Quality Management

Nature and Role of the Elements of CIM System

Nine major elements of a CIM system are in Fig 3 they are,

- Marketing
- Product Design
- Planning
- Purchase
- Manufacturing Engineering
- Factory Automation Hardware
- Warehousing

- Logistics and Supply Chain Management
- Finance
- Information Management

Major elements of CIM systems

i. Marketing: The need for a product is identified by the marketing division. The specifications of the product, the projection of manufacturing quantities and the strategy for marketing the product are also decided by the marketing department. Marketing also works out the manufacturing costs to assess the economic viability of the product.

ii. Product Design: The design department of the company establishes the initial database for production of a proposed product. In a CIM system this is accomplished through activities such as geometric modeling and computer aided design while considering the product requirements and concepts generated by the creativity of the design engineer. Configuration management is an important activity in many designs. Complex designs are usually carried out by several teams working simultaneously, located often in different parts of the world. The design process is constrained by the costs that will be incurred in actual production and by the capabilities of the available production equipment and processes. The design process creates the database required to manufacture the part.

iii. Planning: The planning department takes the database established by the design department and enriches it with production data and information to produce a plan for the production of the product. Planning involves several subsystems dealing with materials, facility, process, tools, manpower, capacity, scheduling, outsourcing, assembly, inspection, logistics etc. In a CIM system, this planning process should be constrained by the production costs and by the production equipment and process capability, in order to generate an optimized plan.

iv. Purchase: The purchase departments is responsible for placing the purchase orders and follow up, ensure quality in the production process of the vendor, receive the items, arrange for inspection and supply the items to the stores or arrange timely delivery depending on the production schedule for eventual supply to manufacture and assembly.

v. Manufacturing Engineering: Manufacturing Engineering is the activity of carrying out the production of the product, involving further enrichment of the database with performance data and information about the production equipment and processes. In CIM, this requires activities like CNC programming, simulation and computer aided scheduling of the production activity. This should include online dynamic scheduling and control based on the real time performance of the equipment and processes to assure continuous production activity. Often, the need to meet fluctuating market demand requires the manufacturing system flexible and agile.

vi. Factory Automation Hardware: Factory automation equipment further enriches the database with equipment and process data, resident either in the operator or the equipment to carry out the production process. In CIM system this consists of computer controlled process machinery such as CNC machine tools, flexible manufacturing systems (FMS), Computer controlled robots, material handling systems, computer controlled assembly systems, flexibly automated inspection systems and so on.

vii. Warehousing: Warehousing is the function involving storage and retrieval of raw materials, components, finished goods as well as shipment of items. In today's complex outsourcing scenario and the need for just-in-time supply of components and subsystems, logistics and supply chain management assume great importance.

viii. Finance: Finance deals with the resources pertaining to money. Planning of investment, working capital, and cash flow control, realization of receipts, accounting and allocation of funds are the major tasks of the finance departments.

ix. Information Management: Information Management is perhaps one of the crucial tasks in CIM. This involves master production scheduling, database management, communication, manufacturing systems integration and management information systems. It can be seen from Fig 4 that CIM technology ties together all the manufacturing and related functions in a company. Implementation of CIM technology thus involves basically integration of all the activities of the enterprise.

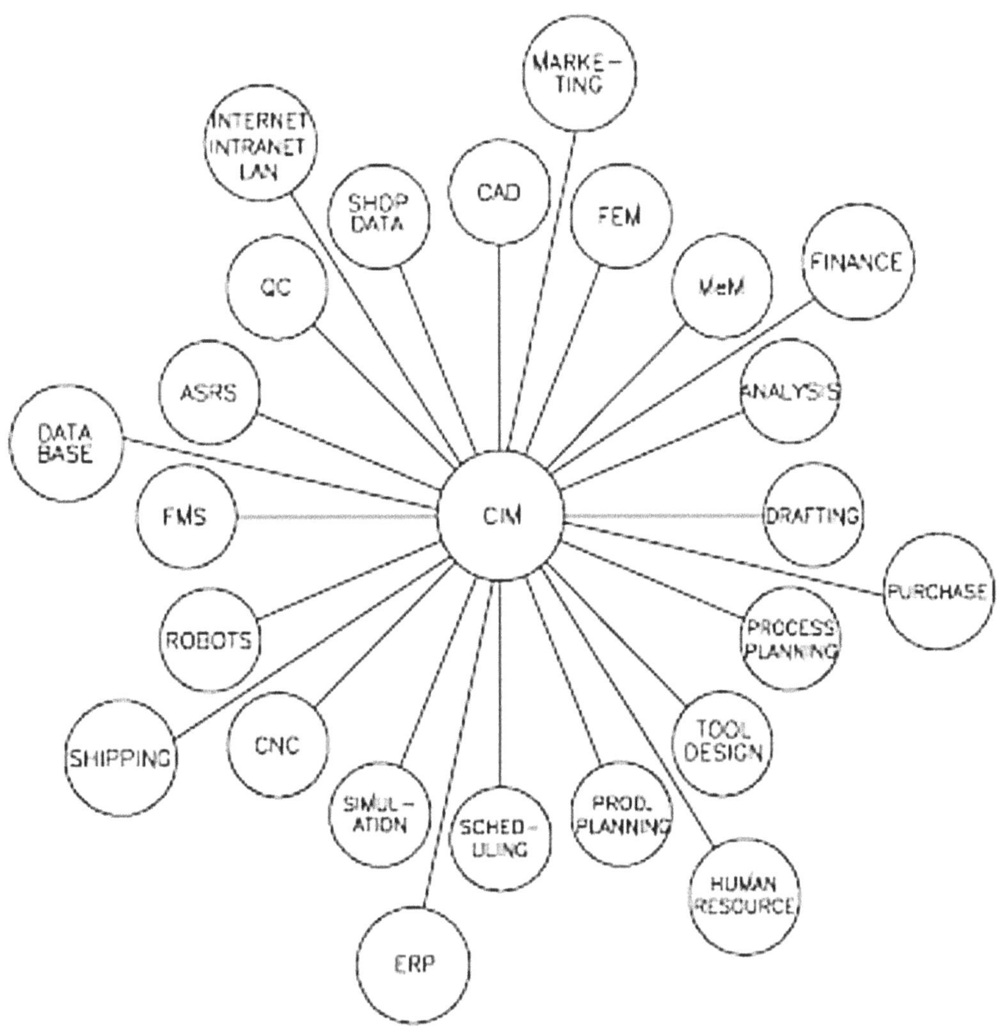

Fig. 4 Various Activities in CIM

The Scope of Computer-Integrated Manufacturing

When all of the activities of the modern manufacturing plants are considered as a whole, it is impossible to think that a small portion might be automated, let alone trying to envisage automation of the whole. In systems approach, a large and complex system with interacting components are analyzed and improved. Anyone vested with the responsibility of implementation of automation for complex system is advised to implement a technique similar to the traditional systems approach.

Following steps are involved in the systems approach:

(a) Objectives of the system are determined.

(b) Structuring the system and set definable system boundaries.

(c) Significant components for a system are determined.

(d) A detailed study of the components is carried out keeping in view the overall integration of the system.

(e) Analyzed components are synthesized into the system.

(f) On the basis of the performance criteria, predetermined system is evaluated.

(g) For continuous improvement, Step „b" to Step "f" are constantly repeated.

No task, however small, should be tackled without knowledge of the task objective. This is the key ingredient which, when lacking, causes members of the same team to pull in different directions. In considering factory automation, there could be many possible objectives. One might be to improve the performance of a specific process. Boundary conditions would then be limited to that process (as well as other processes that might be affected by increased output, such as material supply and assembly after production). Another objective might be to minimize cost in a segment of the operation, while a third might be profit maximization; obviously it is rare that such multiple objectives can all be optimized, even though politicians seem to think so when it comes close to election day. When considering moving to a computer integrated manufacturing operation, the objective would probably be related to being competitive, a problem that manufacturing plants are having at the micro level and a situation that is almost catastrophic for the nation at the macro level.

Setting system boundaries for a CIM project might at first appear to be concerned only with the engineering design and actual manufacture of the products. While the integration of these two components is a major task which is not satisfied in most of the facilities, CIM goes beyond these activities.

Definition of CIM

Joel Goldhar, Dean, Illinois Institute of Technology gives CIM as a computer system in which the peripherals are robots, machine tools and other processing equipment.

Dan Appleton, President, DACOM, Inc. defines CIM is a management philosophy, not a turnkey product.

Jack Conaway, CIM Marketing manager, DEC, defines CIM is nothing but a data management and networking problem. The computer and automated systems association of the society of Manufacturing Engineers (CASA/SEM) defines CIM is the integration of total manufacturing enterprise by using integrated systems and data communication coupled with new managerial philosophies that improve organizational and personnel efficiency.

Dr. J. Harrington, Jr. introduces the concept of Computer Integrated Manufacturing (CIM) in the year 1973. He demonstrated the integration approach to an enterprise. Keeping in mind the current and future market trend for customized product and in order to stand in the competitive edge over long time, virtual organizations are used as an important weapon. Hence, in order to achieve corporate goal and objectives, integration approach is required for customer as well as suppliers. CIM, in general, may be defined as follows:

CIM is the integration of total manufacturing enterprise through the use of integrated system and data communication mixed with new managerial philosophies which results in the improvement of personnel or organizational efficiencies.

From the definition mentioned above, the ultimate goal of CIM is the integration of all the enterprise operation and activities around a common data collection. In this context, society of manufacturing engineers (SME) introduces the CIM wheel, which gives a clear-cut picture of relationship among all parts of the enterprise. Outer layer constitutes of general management which includes marketing, strategic planning, finance, manufacturing management and human resource management. The middle layer consists of three process segments: product and process determination, manufacturing planning and control, and factory automation. These process segments represent all the activities in the design and manufacturing phase of a product life cycle taking the product from concept to assembly. The center of wheel represents the third layer which includes information resources management and common database. Table 1 depicts that fall under the broad purview of the components discussed so far. Table 1 Scope of Computer-Integrated Manufacturing

Operational Flow within CIM

In this section, the operational flow of functions needed to process an item through a manufacturing facility has been briefly discussed. These operation flows within the CAD/CAM environment have been shown by a flow chart (Fig 5). The box number in figure refers the sequence number.

1, 2. All planning must be the function of known customer orders and sales forecasts. If expected demand are not known/or estimated, the enterprise will be working in a vacuum.

3 Management decisions depend on expected orders leading to long-term order requirement that must be satisfied by either production or by subcontracting to outside sources (vendors).

4 A relatively low term evaluation of facility requirement is needed to plan which parts can be manufactured. For example, enough machines of known capacity available, will material be available, can we perform our needs with the current workforce, and so on. The aggregate planning function determines what product quantities should be produced in what time periods to satisfy the long-term requirements. The result of this activity is called the master production schedule or master schedule. It is a schedule for final product, not for the components that go into the final product.

5 The master schedule is affected by current status conditions, so feedback loops come from many sources including problems that might occur with deliveries from vendors, trouble in the shop floor, analysis that reveals demands cannot be satisfied due to capacity problems, lack of vendors, and so on.

6 The material requirements planning (MRP) function takes into consideration the current inventory levels for all components needed to make the final products (a plant might have 20,000 part numbers and perhaps 100 final products for which master schedules have been determined) as well as the components" bills-of-materials and lead time information (obtained from design and process planning data) and evolves component master schedules for all components according to the demand requirements agreed upon. MRP does not take into account whether manufacturing has sufficient capacity to handle the job releases, therefore capacity planning (6a) evaluates shop loading in terms of the requirements and feedback to the master schedule for corrective actions if any problems occur. A further function of MRP based on such analysis is determining whether components should be produced in-house (6b) or subcontracted to outside vendors (6c).

7 Computer aided design is the function that must be completed after a demand for a product has been determined. Thus, the sequence in which it is discussed in this section is not the same as that of sequence or cycle starting from customer to inception through design, manufacturing, assembly and testing, and back to the customer. The design engineer cannot talk in the same terms as the manufacturing engineer. For example, lines, splines, circles, and arcs come under geometrical design whereas pockets chamfer, holes and so on come under manufacturing design. Process planning function is to accomplish the language transition from design to manufacturing.

8 Some of the functions carried out by process planning modules are as:

(a) Sequence of operations required to manufacture a part

(b) Assessing the time requirement to complete the operations.

(c) Determining the type of machines and tooling required.

(d) Enumerate tolerance stacking problems that are credited due to multiple cuts/multiple components related to a part type.

The profitability and non-profitability of a part being manufactured can be ensured by the process planning function because it takes into account the several ways in which a part being manufactured. In order to achieve a detailed schedule, the information related to process planning is fed into MRP analysis and also in the shop floor scheduling (6b). This step may result in the production of a detailed schedule for machines, tooling, fixtures, people and material handling devices, etc. To avoid the damage, all these have to come together at the right time.

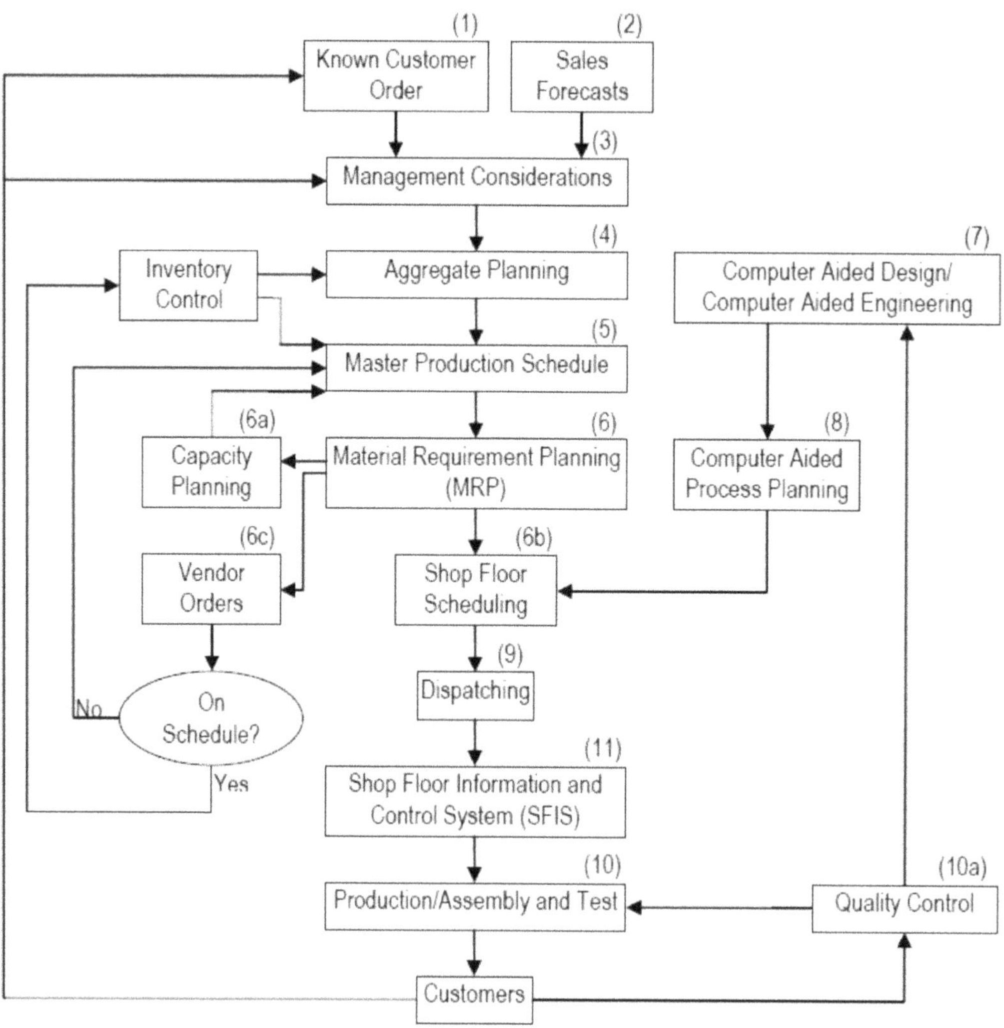

Fig 5: Flow of Operations in CIM

9 Dispatching is the function of releasing all required items needed to perform an operation on a part so that part production must be completed within the schedule time.

10 Production and assembly is accomplished through local control computers and /or programmable controllers. 11. At last, shop floor information system is responsible for getting the required information passed to the downstream entities such as processing equipment, local controllers and sequencing controllers, etc. In this way, real time status records are captured from the various equipments, machines and parts to activate feedback tools so as to ensure the correction or normal continuation of operations in the desired manner.

Computer Aided Manufacturing

The effective use of computer technology in manufacturing planning and control is known as computer aided manufacturing (CAM). Manufacturing engineering functions such as process planning, and numeric control (NC) are included in CAM. The application of CAM is divided in two categories:

(i) Manufacturing planning, and

(ii) Manufacturing control.

Manufacturing Planning

The applications of CAM in manufacturing planning are those in which computers are used directly to support the production function, but there is no direct connection between the computer and the process. The computer is used "offline" to provide information for the effective planning and management of the production activities. The following list surveys the application of CAM in this category:

Computer Aided Process Planning (CAPP)

The route sheets listing the operation sequences and workstations required for manufacturing the products and its components are prepared in process planning. These route sheets are prepared now a days using CAPP.

Computer Assisted NC Part Programming

Computer assisted part programming represents a method to generate the control instructions for the machine tools for complex geometries rather than manual part programming. Part Programming for NC machines is step by step instructions according to which tool movements on the part for metal removal is carried out.

Computerized Machinability Data System

Determination of speed and feed in metal cutting for the given machine tools is a major problem. Computer program is written to propose the suitable condition to use for different materials. Estimation of tool life needs information about material of tools and workpiece, speed, feed and depth of cut etc. As per the cutting conditions, such calculations are to be repeated. Therefore, application of computers for such purposes may assist process planner to a great extent.

Development of Work Standard

Responsibility for setting time standards on direct labour jobs performed in the factory is taken by time study department. It is a very tedious and time-consuming task to establish standards by direct time study. There are several computer packages also available in market for setting up the work standards. These computer programs use standard time data that have been developed for basic work element that comprise any manual task. By summing the times for the individual elements required to perform a new job, the program calculates the standard time for the job.

Cost Estimating

In many industries, cost estimation of a new product is being simplified by computerizing several key steps needed to prepare the estimate. Suitable labour and overhead rates are applied with the help of the computer programs to the sequence of planned operations involved in the components of new products. Individual components cost which range from the engineering bill of the materials to determine the overall product cost is summed up by the program.

Production and Inventory Planning

Extensive application in many of the functions in inventory planning and production control is being executed by the computer. The aforementioned functions are maintenance of inventory records, automatic recording of stock items in the case when inventory is depleted, production scheduling, maintaining current priorities for the different production orders material requirements planning, and capacity planning etc. Computer Aided Line Balancing

It is a very tough job to find the best allocation of work elements among stations on an assembly line if the line is of significant size. The problems are solved with the help of computer program.

Manufacturing Control

Another category of CAM application is development of computer supported system for implementing the manufacturing control functions. These control functions manage and control the physical operation in the factory. These functions are as follows:

Process Monitoring and Control

Process monitoring and control concerned with observing and regulating the production equipment of manufacturing processes in the plant. The applications of the process control are absorbed in automated production system. Which includes the example cases like transfer line assembly system, NC, robotics, material handling and flexible manufacturing systems. All these will be discussed later on. Process monitoring and the control functions are deployed to regulate the actions of various production equipments. Some of the well known control systems used in the industry are as follows.

Quality Control

There are varieties of approaches that insure highest possible quality level in the manufacturing system and products and these are included in quality control.

Shop Floor Control

Production management techniques for collecting data from factory operations and using these data to help control production and inventory in the factory comes under shop floor control. Shop floor control and computerized factory data collection systems are discussed in detail later on.

Inventory Control

The important thing about inventory control is that it maintains the most appropriate level of inventory in the face of two opposing objectives: minimizing the investment and storage cost of holding inventory and maximizing service to customer.

Just in Time Production System

A production system that is planned to deliver exactly the right number of each component to downstream workstations in the manufacturing sequence just at the time when that component is needed is known as just in time production system. This term is applicable to production operation and supplier delivery operation.

Functions of Computer in CIMS

- Machine Control-CNC

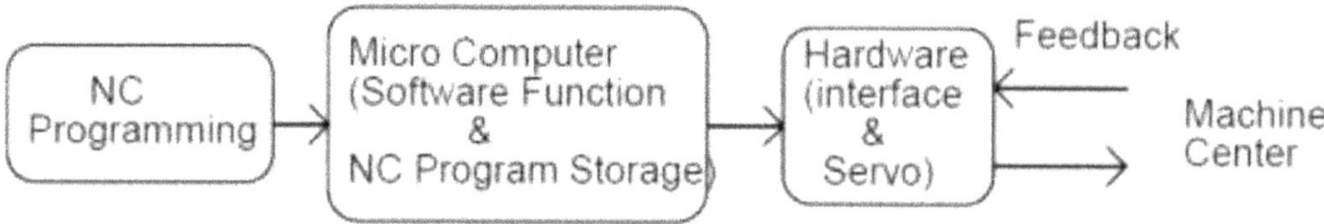

Fig. 6 Schematic diagram of CNC

- Direct Numerical Control (DNC) - Amanufacturing system in which a number of m/c are controlled by a computer through direct connection & in real time.

Consists of 4 basic elements:

- Central computer
- Bulk memory (NC program storage)
- Telecommunication line
- Machine tools (up to 100)

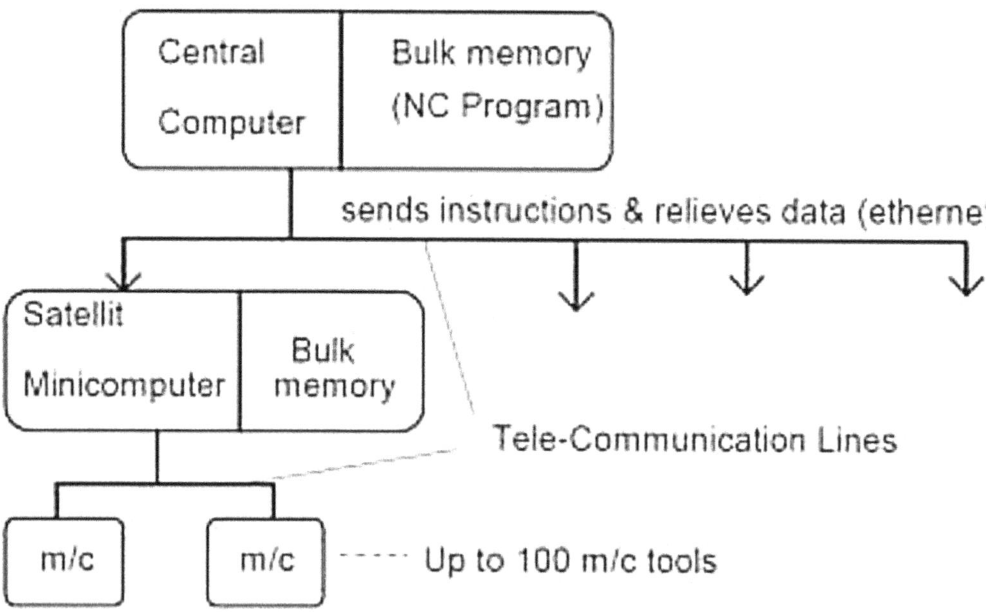

Fig. 7 Schematic representation of Direct Numerical Control

- Production Control - This function includes decision on various parts onto the system.
- Decision is based on:
- production rate/day for the various parts
- Number of raw work parts available

- Number of available pallets
- Traffic & Shuttle Control - Refers to the regulations of the primary & secondary transportation systems which move parts between workstation.
- Work Handling System Monitoring - The computer must monitor the status of each cart & /or pallet in the primary & secondary handling system.
- Tool Control
- Keeping track of the tool at each station
- Monitoring of tool life
- System Performance Monitoring & Reporting - The system computer can be programmed to generate various reports by the management on system performance.
- Utilization reports - summarize the utilization of individual workstation as well as overall average utilization of the system. - Production reports - summarize weekly/daily quantities of parts produced from a CIMS (comparing scheduled production vs. actual production)
- Status reports - instantaneous report "snapshot" of the present conditions of the CIMS.
- Tool reports - may include a listing of missing tool, tool-life status etc.
- Manufacturing data base
- Collection of independent data bases
- Centralized data base
- Interfaced data base
- Distributed data base

Development of CIM

CIM is an integration process leading to the integration of the manufacturing enterprise.

Indicates different levels of this integration that can be seen within an industry. Dictated by the needs of the individual enterprise this process usually starts with the need to interchange information between the some of the so-called islands of automation. Flexible manufacturing cells, automatic storage and retrieval systems, CAD/CAM based design etc. are the examples of islands of automation i.e., a sort of computer based automation achieved completely in a limited sphere of activity of an enterprise. This involves data exchange among computers, NC machines, robots, gantry systems etc. Therefore the integration process has started bottom up. The interconnection of physical systems was the first requirement to be recognized and fulfilled.

The next level of integration, application integration in Fig 6 is concerned with the integration of applications, the term applications being used in the data processing sense. The applications are those which are discussed under the heading CIM hardware and software. Application integration involves supply and retrieval of information, communication between application users and with the system itself. Thus the application integration level imposes constraints on the physical integration level. There has to be control of the applications themselves also.

Benefits of CIM -

There are four basic techniques to determine what the tangible benefits from any capital investment, including CIM, are to a business.

1 Payback period
2 Return on investment.
3 Net present value
4 Internal rate of return. These are traditional financial formulas which management can use to determine the value of CIM to the company. However, the justification process for advanced manufacturing technologies in CIM must be viewed differently from the traditional process for three reasons:
   a) Project Size. CIM investments are projects without ends. Investments made today eventually will be replaced by new technology. Most benefits from CIM accrue with time as advances in both hardware and software take hold.
   b) Project components. Since CIM requires various successful installations of advanced manufacturing technology, benefits will accrue due to the synergism of various pieces on the shop floor. The integration of advanced manufacturing technology long term is what makes CIM a self-liquidating expense.
   c) Identification of CIM soft benefits. The installation of advanced manufacturing technology in a manufacturing environment can provide significant intangible benefits that traditional financial justification methods don't recognize. The benefits most often cited by business executives are reduced manufacturing costs, improved flexibility on the shop floor, responsiveness to the market, improved product quality, improved product design, small lot manufacturing, reduced inventories, and optimal customer service.

While these benefits are hard to quantify, they can reduce operating costs, improve customer relations, and stimulate sales. The key to evaluating these soft benefits is to understand that a CIM environment allows for fewer levels of management and therefore provides for better use of the business's assets, both human and mechanical. The result for the company is improved decision making and significantly improved profitability.

Computer integrated manufacturing, by joining all the functional areas in the business, can provide a variety of automated services in the factory. For businesses to remain competitive, advanced manufacturing technologies must characterize the factory of the future. In this regard, computer integrated manufacturing has many applications:

Order management: CIM allows for faster delivery and responsiveness to customers and to customer orders through electronic data interchange. In essence, customers will electronically secure and lock in supplier capacity for the product. Additionally, a business will be able to respond to inquiries from its customers instantaneously through electronic data interchange. Being able to respond to customers with rapid information will result in extra business, retaining customers, and getting closer to the customer.

Computer-aided design (CAD): Through CAD, CIM allows the computer to assist in minute details and specifications of a customer order or to simulate variations of the order.

Manufacturing resource planning (MRP II): This allows the production schedule to be simulated and integrated using one information base to direct the operations on the plant floor to balance supply and demand.

Computer technology: CIM allows different hardware to be integrated to communicate with one another (open system). It provides a database foundation for both artificial intelligence and expert systems.

Computer-aided manufacturing (CAM): CAM allows for factory machinery to be programmed through numeral controls (NC) tape preparation and computer numerical control (CNC).

Robotics: Robotics allow for the minimization of human activity in the areas of pick/pack, excessive lifting, transportation, and repetitive manufacturing operations.

Automated guided vehicle systems (AGV's). AGV's allow for driverless forklifts and automated storage and retrieval systems. As JIT becomes more imbedded in future manufacturing disciplines, the role of computerized material-bundling equipment will become more vital.

Group technology: Allows for the coding and classification system to group various families of parts or activities, and to aid in both inventory use and part standardization.

Vendor scheduling: CIM provides for improved scheduling of customer orders to improve delivery and internal processing. In the future, orders will be booked directly via electronic data interchange into a vendor's upcoming production schedule. Although this is just a partial list of the uses for computer integrated manufacturing in the factory, it shows that CIM is much more than a means of computers controlling machines.

Principles of CIM

For CIM to be successful businesses must consider the following five fundamental issues involved:

- People and their crucial contribution to manufacturing
- Top management's commitment to the philosophy
- CIM should be put in the context of a well-defined business.
- Strategy or vision
- The technology plan, the system architecture for cim, must
- Include all elements of the company.
- It is extremely important when choosing suppliers to access both
- The breadth and depth of their support capabilities
- People and their crucial contribution to manufacturing -
- "Manufacturing, in general, has not done a very good job of understanding how you link the people and the process into this CIM In the past, CIM projects became automated disasters because management became enamored with the technology and computer side of the program. They completely forgot about the people side and neglected to incorporate people into the development process. Information technology will reshape every company that survives through the 90 s. However, businesses will not be able to incorporate technology advances if they do not find a way to make workers comfortable with computers. Additionally, workers will not have the requisite skills and abilities to succeed and advance if they are not able to work with computers.
- Almost every white-collar job in America requires some level of familiarity with computers. Additionally, it is estimated that 75% of industrial workers also need at least elementary computer skills. Management must understand what enables workers at any skill level to be able to master their computers. Companies that have transformed their work forces with technology have distilled a set of principles that apply equally to workers on an assembly line or in the front office.

These principles include the following:

Think of How to Empower Your Workers, Instead of Dumping

Technology on Them- The most advanced enterprises have realized that they have got to deal with the people side at the same time they deal with the technology.

Listen to Your Employees When Designing a System (Bottom Up) -Managers of highly automated operations are unanimous, if you don't involve the users, you will develop the wrong system. Nobody understands the job like the people who do it. They can tell you how to design the tools that will let them work more efficiently. They will trust new technology more if they had a say in it and knew it was coming. The company wins more commitment from its workers when they feel their contributions were valuable in the design of the system.

Understand and Communicate Your Business Objectives- Employees will accept and learn new technologies if they understand their importance. Fancy computers seldom make much difference in productivity if workers do not understand how the technology helps achieve business goals. It is important to see new technology as only part of a total vision of changed organizations. Therefore, management must look at the information employees need, the materials they need, the incentives they need, and all other aspects of the business, not just automating.

Teach Your Employees by Helping Them Improve Their Performance-The most important aspect of incorporating new technology is learning to do the job better, not learning how to operate the computer. Traditional classroom instruction is seldom the best way to go. The most useful training comes only when workers need it.

Three common approaches are:

a. Mentors, other employees in the organization who know a little more than most, who can help others when questions arise.
b. On-line help programs within the software.
c. Simultaneous interactive video training for workers.

Don't Ignore the Generation Gap - People who grew up in the Nintendo generation have an advantage over their elders. These younger workers adapt more readily to technological incorporation into the workplace. Conversely, big-time computer klutzes may slip in the pecking order if they can't handle the new technology deftly. Some companies introduce workers to computers by using computer games to make them comfortable interacting with a screen. To implement CIM you have to design technology that is usable by people. If people do not use the systems, you might as well throw them away. According to Lee Sage, national director of automotive services at Ernst & Young, "it became apparent that the manufacturing companies that were doing the best job were those that didn't necessarily have the best technology. What they had was a heavy orientation towards people.

Top Management's Commitment to the Philosophy - "The biggest obstacle to CIM implementation...is getting the necessary cross-functional and senior-management support for the fundamental change required to implement CIM across the business. The most important part of successful technological integration is top management commitment and participation. It is estimated that technological illiteracy at the top plagues 90% of American companies. Yet there is no better way to get middle management and supervisors to use computerized tools than to let them see the boss using it first. Therefore, the first worker who has to be brought up to technospeed is the person on top. In many cases, the major stumbling block to implementation of CIM is a lack of familiarity with the technologies at the upper levels of management. "Of the company presidents, chairmen, and CEOs who responded to a Industry Week survey, 58.3% said they are only 'vaguely familiar' with CIM technologies".

CIM should be put in the Context of a Well-Defined Business Strategy or Vision The most important elements of CIM are the business processes and strategies that are developed to support it. They are what drive the whole process. Secondary to all of that is the computer hardware and software. In order for CIM to function properly, it must significantly advance the company's ability to improve quality, increase productivity, provide flexibility in lot sizes and schedules, reduce costs, and help shorten the time it takes to get products designed and to the market. "CIM should never be viewed as being the objective or ultimate goal. The purpose of undertaking the CIM journey is not to have a CIM system. Rather, the purpose of implementing CIM is to help the firm survive by developing a distinctive corporate advantage through its manufacturing capabilities. To this end, CIM requires, as a prerequisite, a well-developed, well understood, and widely known corporate strategy. The entire company needs to be represented in CIM planning. Walls and boundaries between departments and functions must come down. Making CIM an integral part of the overall business strategy and involving people from all parts of the company in planning for CIM will greatly enhance its chances for success. "The thing that most people missed in implementing CIM is the fact that, by itself, CIM isn't enough. The critical missing piece is the concept of an enterprise strategy, which repositions your company to do that which it does best. Many executives are still sorting out their definitions of CIM and its functional role in the overall operation of the business. There has been a gradual shift in thinking in recent years away from a strict technology focus and towards an overall business strategy focus. Managers are asking themselves what are their business objectives and how does CIM fit into these objectives. However, according to an Industry Week Magazine poll, only 32.9% of managers report that their companies have a long-term strategy for implementing CIM. The lack of long-term strategies may have an explanation in the fact that information technologies have been mushrooming at a rapid pace, and manufacturing planners are faced with an unmanageable array of new hardware and software applications. Additionally, the trend toward open-system computing and its implications for selection of computer systems is not fully understood by the top-level executives who will eventually make the go/no-go decisions regarding technology purchases.

The Technology Plan, the System Architecture for CIM, must include all Elements of the Company--The ideal system architecture for CIM will ensure that information can flow where it is needed when it is needed. It must also be flexible enough to be adaptable to the changing needs business and rapidly advancing technologies, while protecting the value of existing investments in the system and technology. Overall, many manufacturing businesses have not been extremely successful at integrating people, processes and functions into an overall CIM concept. "What we are really talking about is going beyond CIM to computer-integrated business management, and hitting on all the key things you need to do to succeed as a business.

It is extremely important when Choosing (Hardware and Software System) Suppliers to Access both The Breadth and depth of their Support Capabilities-- In today's marketplace, a business must look beyond products and pricing when selecting suppliers. Slow start-up, downtime, and other production-related problems cut the very heart out of profitability and can greatly reduce any competitive advantage attained with CIM. Manufacturing companies must look for supplier-support capabilities that include application engineering, training, installation and start-up, coordination with the equipment manufacturer, proper documentation, maintenance, repair-return depots, phone support, on-line system support, and emergency service. Support should be available 24 hours a day, seven days a week, year around. If the company is global, the supplier's ability to support world-wide operations must be taken into consideration prior to the purchase decision.

Objectives and Implementation of a CIM System

The overall job of computer integrated manufacturing strategic planning requires a comprehensive look at the process equipment, facilities, personnel structure and roles, plus the scheduling and control requirements. Implementation of CIM requires the development of a CIM master plan, which encompasses a critical look at the current plant scheduling and control hierarchy (if in an existing facility), a detailed description of the desired plant scheduling and control system hierarchy, and a plan to manage the transition from the current state to the desired future state. This plan must incorporate all functions of the operation (marketing, personnel, engineering, etc.) in their relationships to manufacturing and production control. In order to provide for the overall objectives must be defined of the organization, objectives for the various technology systems expected to be required to meet the business's long-range needs. These systems include database management systems, communications networks, process controls, process optimization, and process improvement and decision support systems. Database management systems should be open in nature and must interconnect, interrelate, and integrate all department and area databases of the business, including corporate, division, research, and marketing strategies, as well as plant operations and production control. Communication networks must provide plant-wide information exchanges with appropriate interactive workstations and permit ready access to plant information by all users of the data. Additionally, they must provide for intra-plant, intradivision, and intra-organization communication as needed. Process control must make computer automated control available in all areas of the manufacturing process. In addition, the technology must expand the scope of conventional control to include the following supporting goals:

a. Minimize the manual entry and recording of all measurements and operational decisions to minimize errors and expedite data acquisition.
b. Simplify the conducting of economic and operational studies to permit quick analysis of unusual operating conditions.
c. Increase the process and system engineer's productivity through readily accessible, efficient and comprehensive analysis and design tools.
d. Increase the scope and interactive access to history data to permit thorough analysis of process and operational problems.
e. Expedite the process of system expansion and growth. Process optimization must permit the expansion of efforts in simulation, optimization, and scheduling of process operations. Process improvement must make use of the available plant-wide information to modify the overall process so as to reduce the number of rejects which are produced.

After completion of the objectives analysis the major steps in the implementation of a CIM system are:

a. Analysis of the existing manufacturing system (if existing plant) or new facility design for compatibility with CIM technology.
b. Analysis of the existing and proposed management and personnel structure for the plant in view of its compatibility with the proposed CIM system.
c. Development of the system master plan for designing and implementing the CIM scheduling and control hierarchy.
d. Develop expected systems costs and project timing in conjunction with systems benefits and projections, thereby establishing justification concerning systems costs and anticipated payout. v. Iterate the steps outlined above until acceptance is obtained from all personnel concerned and company justification criteria is satisfied.
e. Implement and execute system master plan
f. Follow up and adjust as necessary.

Summary: Computer integrated manufacturing (CIM) is a broad term covering all technologies and soft automation used to manage the resources for cost effective production of tangible goods.

- Integration - capital, human, technology and equipment
- CIM - This orchestrates the factors of production and its management.

Computer Aided Design (CAD)

Computer Aided Manufacturing (CAM)

Flexible Manufacturing Systems (FMS)
Computer Aided Process Planning (CAPP)

- CIM is being projected as a panacea for Discrete manufacturing type of industry, which produces 40% of all goods.

"CIM is not applying computers to the design of the products of the company. That is computer aided design (CAD)! It is not using them as tools for part and assembly analysis. That is computer aided engineering (CAE)! It is not using computers to aid the development of part programs to drive machine tools. That is computer aided manufacturing (CAM)! It is not materials requirement planning (MRP) or just-in-time (JIT) or any other method of developing the production schedule. It is not automated identification, data collection, or data acquisition. It is not simulation or modeling of any materials handling or robots or anything else like that. Taken by themselves, they are the application of computer technology to the process of manufacturing. But taken by themselves they only crate the islands of automation."

- Leo Roth Klein, Manufacturing Control systems, Inc.

Definition of CIM

It describes integrated applications of computers in manufacturing. A number of observers have attempted to refine its meaning:

One needs to think of CIM as a computer system in which the peripherals, instead of being printers, plotters, terminals and memory disks are robots, machine tools and other processing equipment. It is a little noisier and a little messier, but it's basically a computer system.

- Joel Goldhar, Dean, Illinois Institute of Technology

CIM is a management philosophy, not a turnkey computer product. It is a philosophy crucial to the survival of most manufacturers because it provides the levels of product design and production control and shop flexibility to compete in future domestic and international markets.

- Dan Appleton,

President, DACOM, Inc.

CIM is an opportunity for realigning your two most fundamental resources: people and technology. CIM is a lot more than the integration of mechanical, electrical, and even informational systems. It's an understanding of the new way to manage.

- Charles Savage, president, Savage Associates CIM is nothing but a data management and networking problem.

- Jack Conaway, CIM marketing manager, DEC The preceding comments on CIM have different emphases (as highlighted).

An attempt to define CIM is analogous to a group of blind persons trying to describe an elephant by touching it.

"CIM is the integration of the total manufacturing enterprise through the use of integrated systems and data communications coupled with new managerial philosophies that improve organizational and personnel efficiency."

- Shrensker, Computer Automated Systems Association of the Society of Manufacturing Engineers (CASA/SME)

Concept or Technology

"Some people view CIM as a concept, while others merely as a technology. It is actually both. A good analogy of CIM is man, for what we mean by the word man presupposes both the mind and the body. Similarly, CIM represents both the concept and the technology. The concept leads to the technology which, in turn, broadens the concept."

- According to Vajpayee

The meaning and origin of CIM

The CIM will be used to mean the integration of business, engineering, manufacturing and management information that spans company functions from marketing to product distribution.

The changing and manufacturing and management scenes

The state of manufacturing developments aims to establish the context within which CIM exists and to which CIM must be relevant. Agile manufacturing, operating through a global factory or to world class standards may all operate alongside CIM. CIM is deliberately classed with the technologies because, as will be seen, it has significant technological elements. But it is inappropriate to classify CIM as a single technology, like computer aided design or computer numerical control.

External communications

Electronic data interchange involves having data links between a buying company's purchasing computer and the ordering computer in the supplying company. Data links may private but they are more likely to use facilities provided by telephone utility companies.

Islands of automation and software

In many instances the software and hardware have been isolated. When such computers have been used to control machines, the combination has been termed an island of automation. When software is similarly restricted in its ability to link to other software, this can be called an island of software.

Dedicated and open systems

The opposite of dedicated in communication terms is open. Open systems enable any type of computer system to communicate with any other.

Manufacturing automation protocol (MAP)

The launch of the MAP initiates the use of open systems and the movement towards the integrated enterprise.

Product related activities of a company

- Marketing
- Sales and customer order serviceing

Engineering

- Research and product development
- Manufacturing development
- Design
- Engineering release and control
- Manufacturing engineering
- Facilities engineering
- Industrial engineering

Production planning

- Master production scheduling
- Material planning and resource planning
- Purchasing
- Production control

Plant operations

- Production management and control
- Material receiving

- Storage and inventory
- Manufacturing processes - Test and inspection
- Material transfer
- Packing, dispatch and shipping
- Plant site service and maintenance

Physical distribution

- Physical distribution planning
- Physical distribution operations
- Warranties, servicing and spares

Business and financial management

- Company services
- Payroll
- Accounts payable, billing and accounts receivable

Introduction to Process Planning

Process planning is concerned with determining the sequence of individual manufacturing operations needed to produce a given part or product. The resulting operation sequence is documented on a form typically referred to as operation sheet. The operation sheet is a listing of the production operations and associated machine tools for a work part or assembly. Process planning is an important stage of product development since production tooling like jigs, fixtures, special tools etc. can be designed only after the process is finalized.

Role of process planning

1 Interpretation of product design data
2 Selection of machining processes.
3 Selection of machine tools.
4 Determination of fixtures and datum surfaces.
5 Sequencing the operations.
6 Selection of inspection devices.
7 Determination of production tolerances.
8 Determination of the proper cutting conditions.

9 Calculation of the overall times.
10 Generation of process sheets including NC data.

Approaches to Process planning.

1 Manual approach
2 Variant or retrieval type CAPP system
3 Generative CAPP system

Process Planning

Manufacturing planning, process planning, material processing, process engineering and machine routing are a few titles given to the topic referred to here as process planning. Process planning is that function within a manufacturing facility that establishes which machining process and process parameters are to be used to convert a work material (blank) from its initial form (raw material) to a final form defined by an engineering drawing. Process planning is a common task in small batch, discrete parts metal working industries. The process planning activity can be divided into the following steps:

- Selection of processes and tools
- Selection of machine tools/Manufacturing equipment
- Sequencing the operations
- Grouping of operations
- Selection of work piece holding devices and datum surfaces (set ups)
- Selection of inspection instruments
- Determination of production tolerances
- Determination of the proper cutting conditions
- Determination of the cutting times and non-machining times (setting time, inspection time) for each operation
- Editing the process sheets.

All the information determined by the process planning function is recorded on a sheet called process plan. The process plan is frequently called an operation sheet, route sheet or operation planning sheet. This provides the instructions for the production of the part. It contains the operation sequence, processes, process parameters and machine tools used.

In conventional production system, a process plan is created by a process planner. It requires a significant amount of time and expertise to determine an optimal routing for each new part design. However, individual engineers will have their own opinions about what constitutes the best routing. Accordingly, there are differences among the operation sequences developed by various planners. Efficient process planning requires the service of experienced process planners.

Because of the problems encountered with manual process planning, attempts have been made in recent years to capture the logic, judgment and experience required for this important function and incorporates them into computer programmes. Based on the features of a given part, the program automatically generates the sequence of manufacturing operations. The process planning software provides the opportunity to generate production routings which are rational, consistent and perhaps even optimal.

It has the following advantages:

i. Reduces the skill required of a planner.

ii. Reduces the process planning time.

iii. Reduces the process planning and manufacturing cost.

iv. Creates more consistent plans.

v. Produces more accurate plans.

vi. Increases productivity.

The current approaches for computer aided process planning can be classified into two groups:

i. Variant

ii. Generative

Structure of a Process Planning Software

Fig. 10 represents the structure of a computer aided process planning system. In Fig. 10 the modules are not necessarily arranged in the proper sequence but can be based on importance or decision sequence. Each module may require execution several times in order to obtain the optimum process plan. The input to the system will most probably be a solid model from a CAD data base or a 2-D model. The process plan after generation and validation can then be routed directly to the production planning system and production control system.

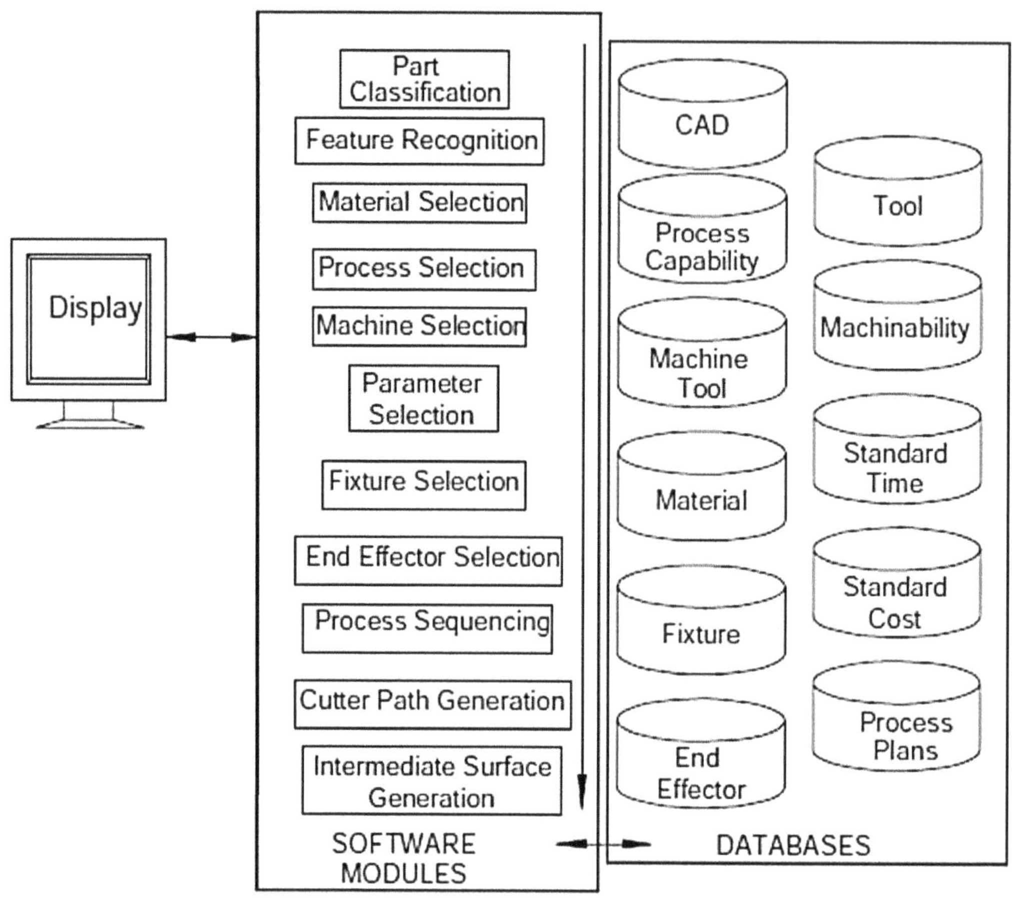

Fig. 10 Structure of a Computer Aided Process Planning System

Information required for Process Planning

The geometric model of the part is the input for the process planning system. The system outputs the process plan (Fig. 11). The input to the process planning system may be engineering drawing or CAD model.

The other prerequisites for process planning are given below:

- Parts list
- Annual demand/batch size
- Accuracy and surface finish requirement (CAD Database)
- Equipment details (Work centre Database)
- Data on cutting fluids, tools, jigs & fixtures, gauges
- Standard stock sizes
- Machining data, data on handling and setup

Fig. 11 Activities in Process Planning

In a computerized process planning system a formal structure and a knowledge database are required in order to transform the engineering design information into the process definition. A brief description of the operation of a computer aided process planning software is given in the following section.

Methods of Computer Aided Process Planning

The ultimate goal of a system is to integrate design and production data into a system that generates useable process plans. As already mentioned there are two approaches:

i. Variant process planning

ii. Generative process planning

Variant Process Planning

A variant process planning system uses the similarity among components to retrieve the existing process plans. A process plan that can be used by a family of components is called a standard plan. A standard plan is stored permanently with a family number as its key. A family is represented by a family matrix which includes all possible members. The variant process planning system has two operational stages:

- A preparatory stage and
- A production stages.

During the preparatory stage, existing components are coded, classified, and subsequently grouped into families. The process begins by summarizing process plans already prepared for components in the family. Standard plans are then stored in a data base and indexed by family matrices (Fig. 12).

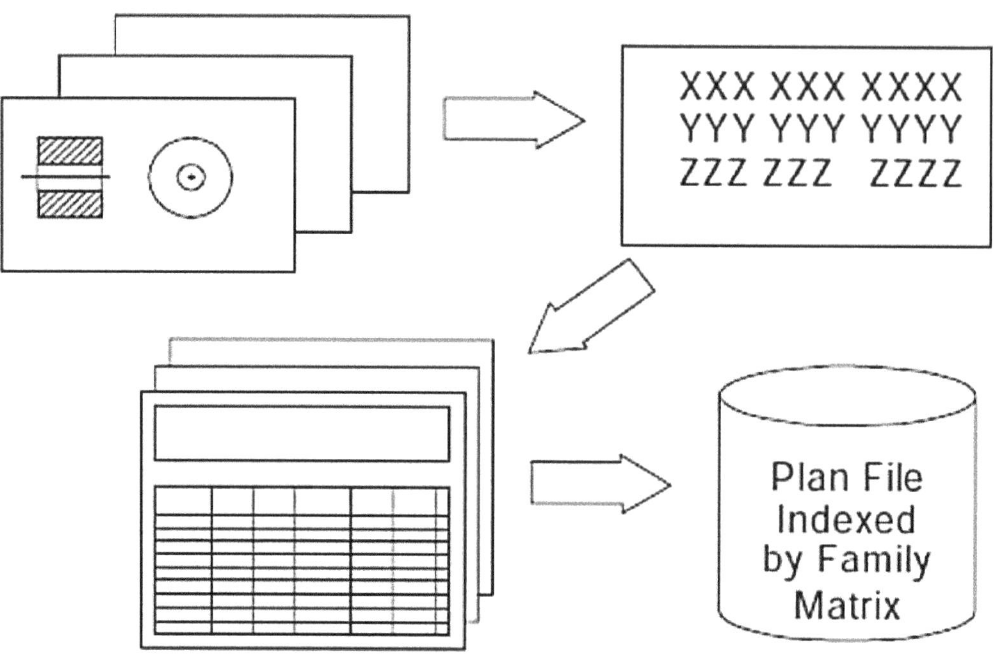

Fig. 12 Process Family Matrix

The operation stage occurs when the system is ready for production. An incoming part is first coded. The code is then input to a part family search routine to find the family to which the component belongs. The family number is then used to retrieve a standard plan. Some other functions, such as parameter selection and standard time calculations, can also be added to make the system more complete (Fig. 13). This system is used in a machine shop that produces a variety of small components.

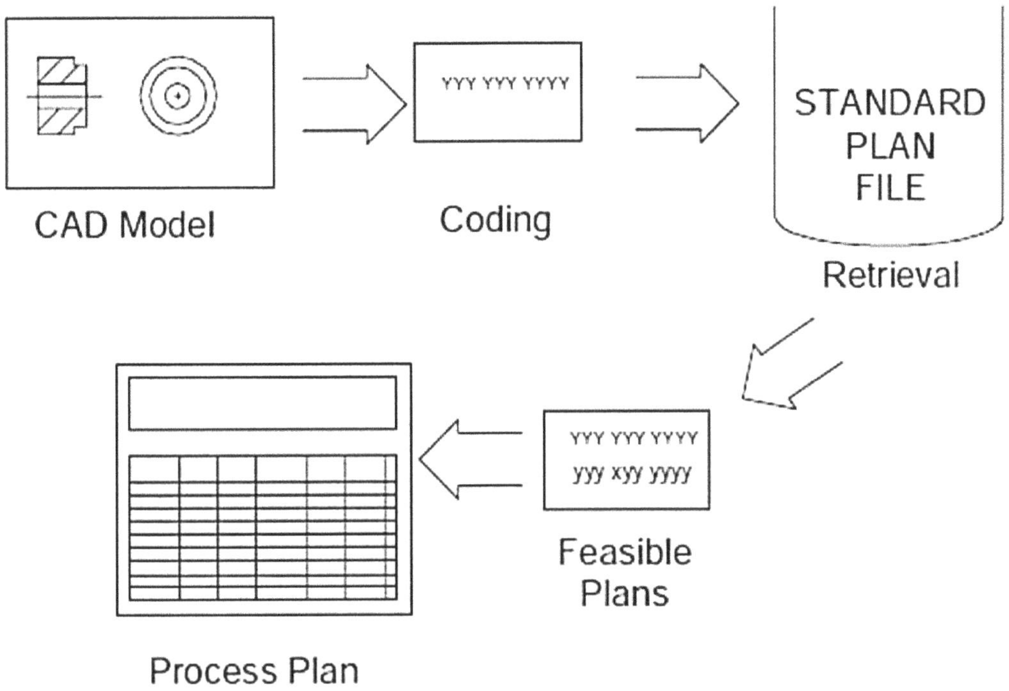

Fig. 13 Part Search and Retrieval

Design of Variant Process Planning System

The following are the sequences in the design of a variant process planning system:

i. Family formation

ii. Data base structure design iii. Search algorithm development and implementation

iv. Plan editing.

v. Process parameter selection/updating.

Family Formation

Part family classification and coding were discussed earlier. This is based on the manufacturing features of a part. Components requiring similar processes are grouped into the same family. A general rule for part family formation is that all parts must be related. Then, a standard process plan can be shared by the entire family. Minimum modification on the standard plan will be required for such family members.

Data Base Structure Design

The data base contains all the necessary information for an application, and can be accessed by several programs for specific application. There are three approaches to construct a data base: hierarchical, network, and relational.

Search Procedure

The principle of a variant system is to retrieve process plans for similar components. The search for a process plan is based on the search of a part family to which the component belongs. When, the part family is found, the associated standard plan can then be retrieved. A family matrix search can be seen as the matching of the family with a given code. Family matrices can be considered as masks. Whenever, a code can pass through a mask successfully, the family is identified.

Plan Editing and Parameter Selection

Before a process plan can be issued to the shop, some modification of the standard plan may be necessary, and process parameters must be added to the plan. There are two types of plan editing: One is the editing of the standard plan itself in the data base, and the other is editing of the plan for the component. For editing a standard plan, the structure of the data base must be flexible enough for expansion, additions, and deletions of the data records. A complete process plan includes not only operations but also process parameters. The data in the process parameter files are linked so that we can go through the tree to find the speed and feed for an operation. The parameter file can be integrated into variant planning to select process parameters automatically.

Generative Process Planning

Generative process planning is a system that synthesizes process information in order to create a process plan for a new component automatically. In a generative planning system, process plans are created from information available in manufacturing data base without human intervention. Upon receiving the design model, the system can generate the required operations and operation sequences for the component. Knowledge of manufacturing must be captured and encoded into efficient software. By applying decision logic, a process planner's decision making can be imitated. Other planning functions, such as machine selection, tool selection, process optimization, and so on, can also be automated using generative planning techniques.

The generative planning has the following advantages:

i. It can generate consistent process plans rapidly.

ii. New process plans can be created as easily as retrieving the plans of existing components.

iii. It can be interfaced with an automated manufacturing facility to provide detailed and up-to-date control information.

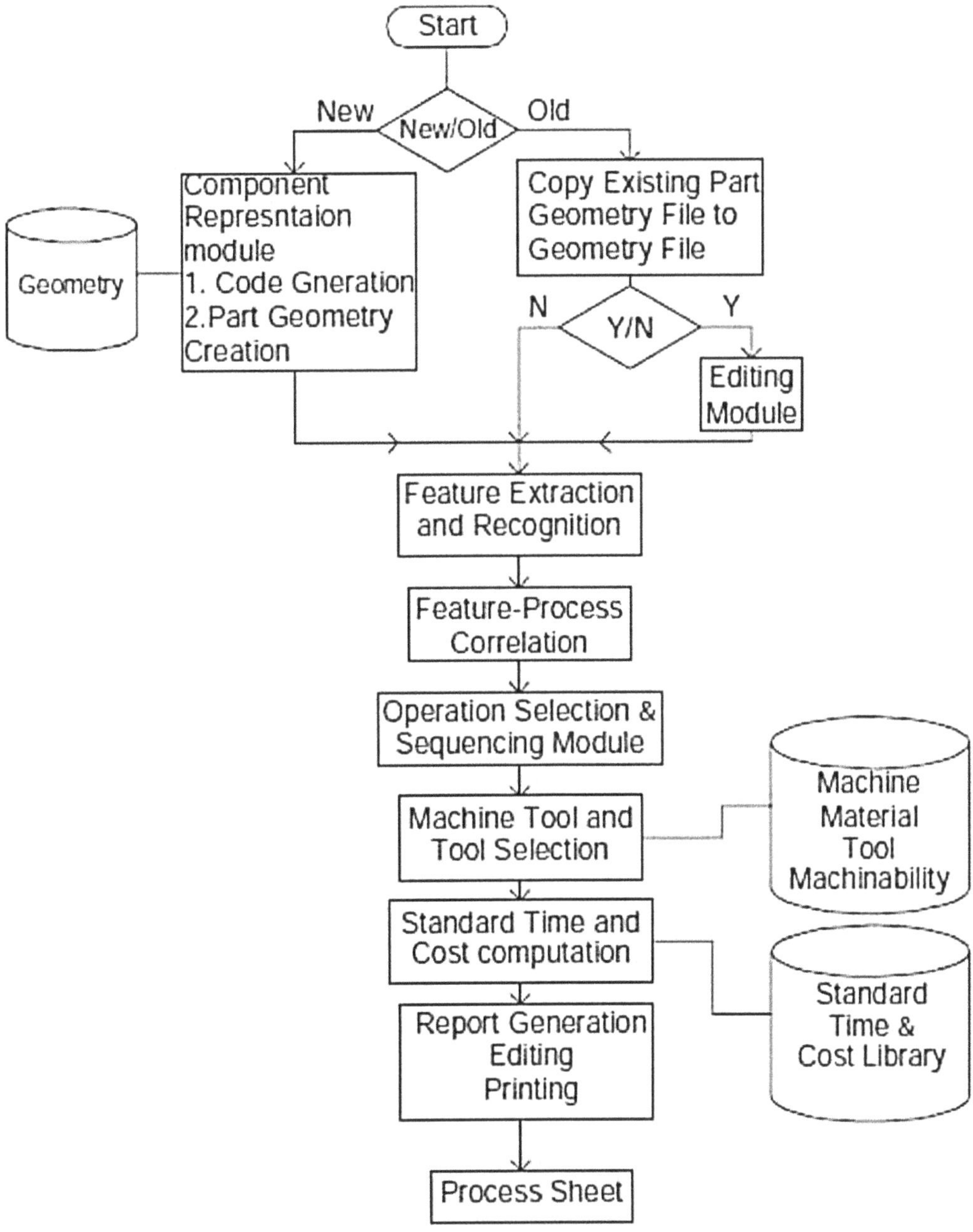

Fig. 14 shows the modular structure of a generative CAPP system.

The generative part consists of:

- Component representation module
- Feature extraction module
- Feature process correlation module
- Operation selection and sequencing module
- Machine tool selection module
- Standard time / cost computation module
- Report generation module

In order to generate a more universal process planning system, variables such as process limitations, and capabilities, process costs and so on, must be defined at the planning stage. Several of methods have been proposed for creating generative process plans. A few methods that have been implemented successfully are:

i. Forward and backward planning

ii. Input Format

iii. CAPP based on CAD models.

iv. CAPP based on decision logic either using decision trees or decision tables.

v. CAPP based on artificial intelligence.

Forward and Backward Planning

In generative process planning, when process plans are generated, the system must define an initial state in order to reach the final state (goal). The path taken represents the sequence of processes. For example, the initial state is the raw material and the final state is the component design. Then a planner works in modifying the raw workpiece until it takes on the final design qualities. This is called forward planning. Backward planning uses a reverse procedure. Assuming that we have a finished component, the goal is to go back to the un-machined workpiece. Each machining process is considered a filling process. Forward and backward planning may seem similar. However they influence the programming of the system significantly. Planning each process can be characterized by a precondition of the surface to be machined and a post condition of the machining (the end result). For forward planning, we must know the successor surface before we select a process, because the post condition of the first process becomes the precondition for second process. Backward planning eliminates this problem since it begins with the final surfaces from and processes are selected to satisfy the initial requirements. In forward planning, the steps to obtain the final surface with the desirable attributes must be carefully planned to guarantee the result. On the other hand, backward planning starts with the final requirements and searches for the initial condition.

Process Planning Systems

The majority of existing process planning systems is based on variant process planning approach. Some of them are: CAPP, MIPLAN, MITURN, MIAPP, UNIVATION, CINTURN, COMCAPPV, etc. However, there are some generative system, such as METCAPP, CPPP, AUTAP, and APPAS. Some of the planning systems are discussed in the following paragraph. These are systems continuously evolving in many cases. The descriptions are therefore only approximate.

CAM-I CAPP

The CAM-I (Computer Aided Manufacturing-International) system (CAPP) is perhaps the most widely used of all process planning systems. CAPP is a database management system written in ANSI standard FORTRAN. It provides a structure for a data base, retrieval logic, and interactive editing capability. The coding scheme for part classification and the output format are added by the user. PI-CAPP, an extension of CAPP, has its own (built-in) coding and classification system. This eliminates the requirement of a user developed coding scheme. A typical CAPP system is shown in Fig. 15.

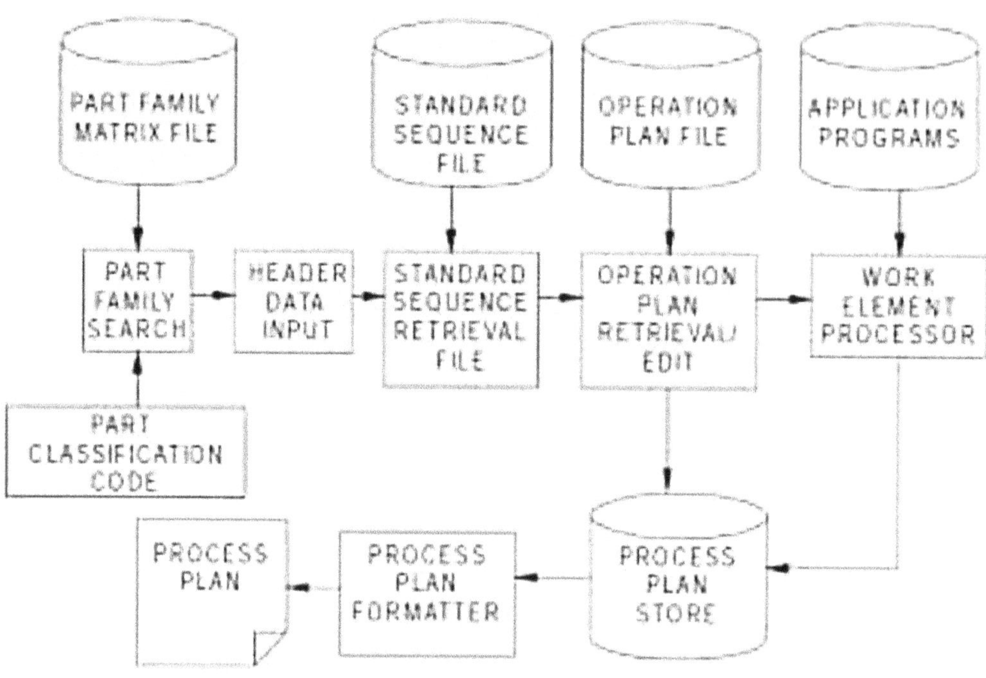

Fig. 15 CAPP System

Miplan And Multicapp

Both MIPLAN and MULTICAPP were developed in conjunction with OIR (Organization for Industrial Research). They are both variant systems that use the MICLASS coding system for part description. They are data retrieval systems which retrieve process plans based on part code, part number, family matrix, and code range. By inputting a part code, parts with a similar code are retrieved. The process plan for each part is then displayed and edited by the user. A typical MULTICAPP system is shown in Fig. 16.

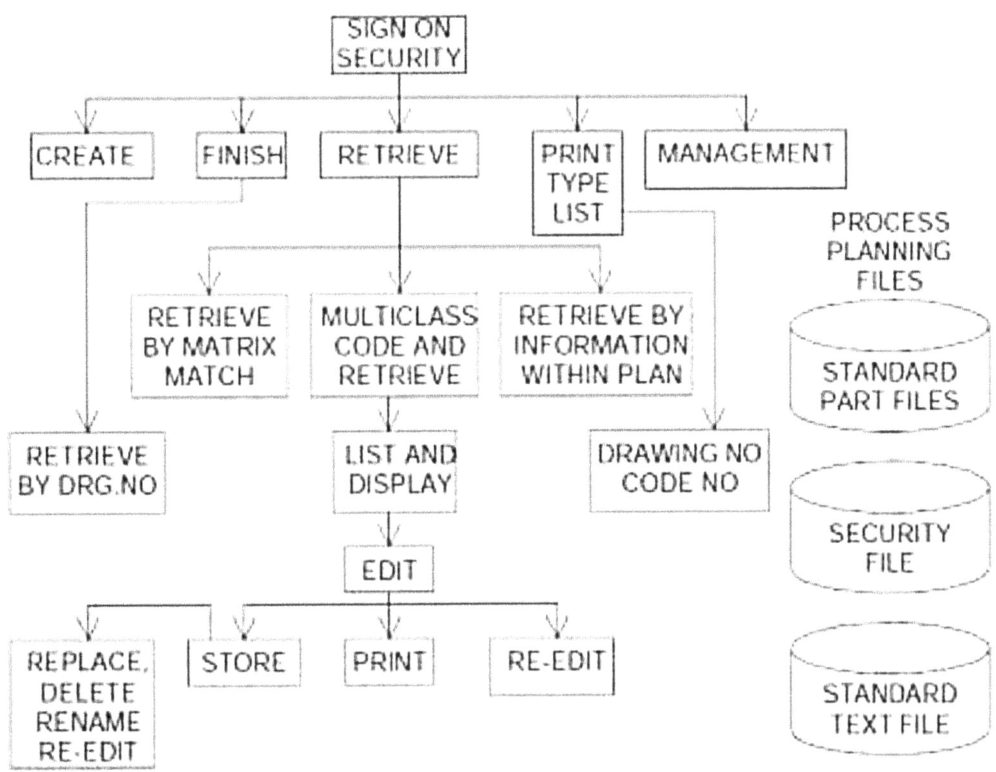

Fig. 16 MULTICAPP System

APPAS and CADCAM

APPAS is a generative system for detailed process selection. CADCAM is an example of APPAS. CADCAM operates using a CAD "front end" to interface with APPAS. APPAS describes the detailed technological information of each machined surface by means of a special code. CADCAM provides an interactive graphics interface to APPAS. Components can be modeled graphically and edited interactively.

AUTOPLAN and RPO

AUTOPLAN is generative only in the detailing of the part. The process selection and process sequencing level do not differ significantly from CAPP or MIPLAN. The four major modules of the system are:

i. Group technology retrieval-process plan retrieval.

ii. Graphical planning aides- tooling layout, verification and work instruction and preparation.

iii. Generative process planning.

iv. Process optimization.

AUTAP System

The AUTAP system is one of the most complete planning systems in use today. AUTAP uses primitives to construct a part similar to a constructive solid geometry (CSG). AUTAP is a system designed especially to interface with a CAD system. It can be installed as part of an integrated CAD/CAM system.

CPPP

CPPP (computerized production process planning) was designed for planning cylindrical parts. CPPP is capable of generating a summary of operations and the detailed operation sheets required for production. The principle behind CPPP is a composite component concept. A composite component can be thought of as an imaginary component which contains all the features of components in one part family. CPPP incorporates a special language, COPPL, to describe the process model. CPPP allows an interactive mode whereby the planner can interact with the system at several fixed interaction points.

GARI

GARI is an experimental problem solver which uses artificial intelligence (AI) techniques. The unique feature of the GARI is the representation of planning knowledge. GARI employs a production rule knowledge base to store process capabilities.

TIPPS

Although the process planning steps have been discussed, an integrated approach to generative process planning has yet to be presented. TIPPS is acronym for Totally Integrated Process planning. TIPPS is generative process planning system that has evolved from the APPAS and CAD/CAM systems. In TIPPS, the logical divisions of process planning are broken into functional modules. TIPPS has the following features:

- It has a modular structure.
- It can interact with a CAD system.
- It allows for interactive surface identification.
- It contains a process/knowledge description language.

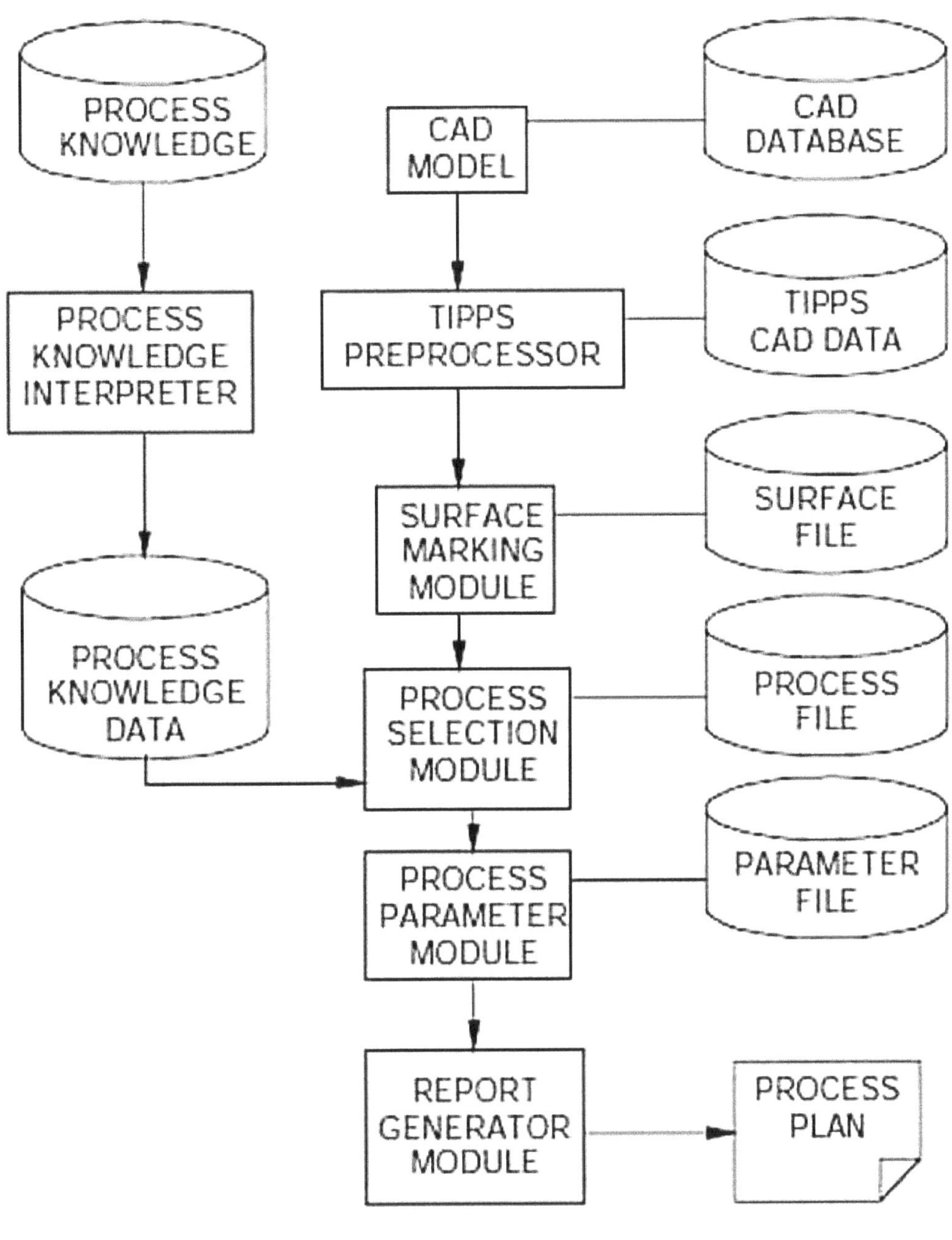

Fig. 17 TIPPS

Process planning with the aid of computer.

- Process planning is concerned with the preparation of route sheets that list the sequence of operations and work centers require to produce the product and its components.
- Manufacturing firms try to automate the task of process planning using CAPP systems duc to many limitations of manual process planning. These includes:
- Tied to personal experience

- and knowledge of planner of production facilities, equipment, their capabilities, process and tooling. This results in inconsistent plans.
- Manual process planning is time consuming and slow.
- Slow in responding to changes in product design and production.
- The experience of manufacturing of different engineers, who are likely to retire, can be made available in future by CAPP.
- CAPP is usually considered to be part of CAM, however this results CAM as standalone system. - Synergy of CAM can be achieved by integrating it with CAD system and CAPP acts as a connection between the two.
- Readymade CAPP systems are available today to prepare route sheets.

Benefits derived from CAPP

- Process rationalization and standardization
- Increased productivity of process planners
- Reduced lead time for process planning
- Improved legibility
- Incorporation of other application programs

Design approaches of CAPP systems

Retrieval CAPP systems/ Variant CAPP

- This has evolved out of the traditional manual process planning method. A process plan for a new part is created by identifying and retrieving an existing plan for a similar part, followed by the necessary modifications to adapt it to the new part.

- It is based on GT principles, i.e., part classification and coding. These coding allow the CAPP system to select a baseline process plan for the part family and accomplish about 90% of the planning work. The planner adds the remaining 10% of the planning by modifying the baseline plan.

- If the code of the part does not match with the codes stored in the database, a new process plan must be generated manually and then entered into database to create a new baseline process plan for future use.

Advantages and limitations of Variant CAPP

- Investment in hardware and software is not much.
- The system offers a shorter development time and lower manpower consumption to develop process plan.
- The system is very reliable and reasonable in real production environments for small and medium size companies.
- Quality of process plan depends on knowledge and background of process planner.

Generative CAPP

- Process plans are generated by means of decision logics, formulas, algorithms, and geometry based data that are built or fed as input to the system.
- Format of input
- Text input (interactive)
- Graphical input (from CAD models)
- First key: to develop decision rules appropriate for the part to be processed. These rules are specified using decision trees, logical statements, such as if-then-else, or artificial intelligence approaches with object-oriented programming.
- Second key: Finding out the data related to part to drive the planning. Simple forms of generative CAPP systems may be driven by GT codes.

A pure generative system can produce a complete process plan from part classification and other design data which does not require any further modification or manual interaction.

- In generating such plans, initial state of the part (stock) must be defined in order to reach the final state i.e., finished part.
- Forward or backward planning can be done.
- Forward and backward planning apparently appear to be similar but they effect programming significantly. The requirement and the results in of a setup in forward

planning are the results and requirements, respectively, of the set up in backward planning.

- Forward planning suffers from conditioning problems; the results of a setup affect the next set up.
- In backward planning, conditioning problems are eliminated because setups are selected to satisfy the initial requirements only.
- The generative CAPP has all the advantages of variant CAPP however it has an additional advantage that it is fully automatic and a up-to-date process plan is generated at each time.
- It requires major revisions if a new equipment or processing capabilities became available.
- The development of the system in the beginning is a difficult What is CAPP?

Process planning acts as a bridge between design and manufacturing by translating design specifications into manufacturing process details.

Process Plan

- Refers to a set of instructions that are used to make a component or a part so that the design specifications are met.
- Determines how a component will be manufactured.
- Is a major determinant of manufacturing cost and profitability of products

Process Planning

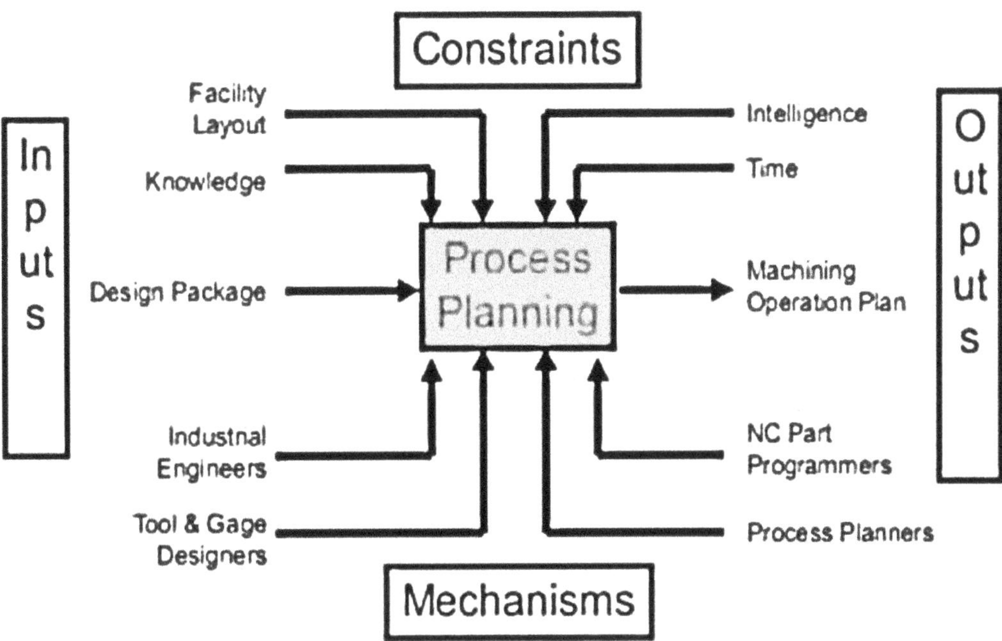

Fig. 21 working principle of Process Planning Basic Process in developing a process plan

1 Analysis of part requirements

2 Selection of raw workpiece

3 Determining manufacturing operations and their sequence

4 Selection of machine tools

5 Selection of tools, work-holding devices, and inspection equipment

6 Determining machining conditions (cutting speed, feed, depth of cut) and manufacturing times (setup time, processing time, and lead times)

- Process Planning Approaches
- Manual Systems
- Computer Aids

Variant System

Experimental Generative System

Manually Prepared Process Plans

- A skilled individual examines a part drawing to develop the necessary instructions for the process plan
- Requires knowledge of the manufacturing capabilities of the factory (many times undocumented)
- Machine and process capabilities, tooling, materials, standard practices, and associated costs
- Widely used, time consuming, plans developed over a period of time may not be consistent nor objective
- Excessive time and cost may be required to develop necessary skills for successful planners Computer Aids
- "Computer-aided" is a key factor in the integration of CAD and CAM
- The use of computers in process planning can:
- Systematically produce accurate and consistent process plans
- Reduce the cost and lead time of process planning
- Reduce skill requirements of process planners
- Increase productivity of process planners
- Interface application programs such as work standards, cost estimation, and lead time estimation
- Consistently optimize process routings
- Reduce preproduction lead times
- Increase responsiveness to engineering changes

Variant (Retrieval) CAPP Methodology

- Recall, identify, and retrieve and existing plan for a similar part and make necessary modifications.
- Interactive environment between the planner and the computer
- Process planning for a new part starts with coding and classifying the part into a similar family.
- Requires the establishment and maintaining of a database of standard process plans that contains operations, tools, notes, etc.
- Requires recall and editing capability

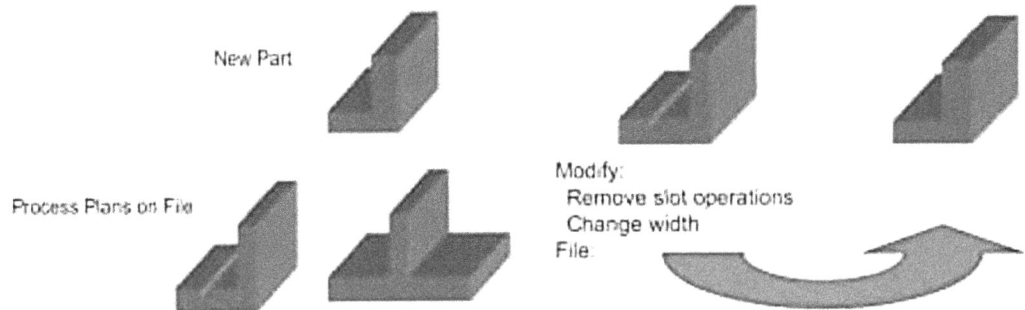

Fig. 22 Variant (Retrieval) CAPP Methodology

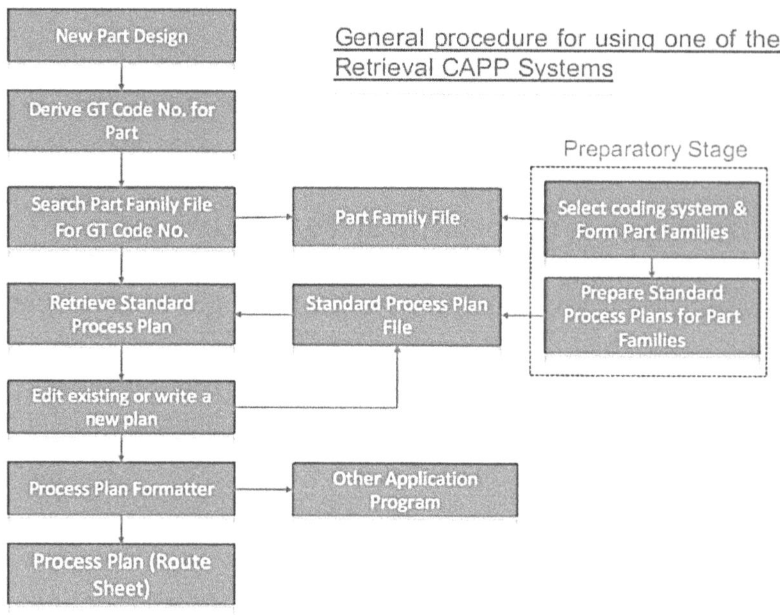

Fig. 23 Variant (Retrieval)

CAPP Methodology

Fig. 23 Variant CAPP procedure

- Advantages:
- Efficient processing and evaluation of complicated activities and decisions
- Standardized procedures
- Lower development and hardware costs
- Shorter development times
- Disadvantages:
- Inconsistency in editing
- Quality is dependent on knowledge and skill of planner
- Optimization of variables such as material, geometry, size, precision, quality, alternative processing sequences, and machine loading is difficult Generative CAPP Methodology

- Process plans are automatically generated by means of decision logic, formulae, technology algorithms, and textual and geometry-based data
- Truly universal system not yet developed
- There are essentially two major components
- Geometry-based -- define all geometric features for all process related surfaces together with feature dimensions, locations, and tolerances and the surface finish desired on the features.
- Knowledge-based -- the automatic matching of part geometry requirements with the manufacturing capabilities using process knowledge in the form of decision logic and data.

Knowledge based process planning

- Knowledge-based; Artificial Intelligence; Expert System; Rule-based...
- "Mimic the decision-making process of a human expert"
- Experience → Knowledge
- Human experts "learns" → How about software?
- Knowledge Representation:

IF < CONDITIONS > THEN < ACTION >

Decision Tables

A table of rows and columns, separated into four quadrants

- Conditions
- Condition alternatives
- Actions to be taken
- Rules for executing the actions The standard format used for presenting a decision table

- Conditions and Actions
- Conditions
- Actions Rules
- Condition Alternatives
- Action Entries

Developing Decision Tables

- Determine conditions that affect the decision
- Determine possible actions that can be taken
- Determine condition alternatives for each condition
- Calculate the maximum number of columns in the decision table
- Fill in the condition alternatives
- Complete table by inserting an X where rules suggest actions
- Combine rules where it is apparent
- Check for impossible situations
- Rearrange to make more understandable

MULTIPLE CHOICE QUESTIONS

1. During the execution of a CNC part program block NO20 GO2 X45.0 Y25.0 R5.0 the type of tool motion will be
a) circular Interpolation – clockwise
b) circular Interpolation – counterclockwise
c) linear Interpolation
d) rapid feed

Answer: a
Explanation: Given: -NO20 GO2 X45.0 Y25.0 R5.0
Here term X45.0 Y25.0 R5.0 will produce circular motion because radius is consider in this term and GO2 will produce clockwise motion of the tool.

2. In an NC machining operation, the tool has to be moved from point (5, 4) to point (7, 2) along a circular path with centre at (5, 2). Before starting the operation, the tool is at (5, 4). The correct G and N codes for this motion are
a) N010GO3X7.0Y2.0I5.0J2.0
b) N010GO2X7.0Y2.0I5.0J2.0
c) N010GO1X7.0Y2.0I5.0J2.0
d) N010GOOX7.0Y2.0I5.0J2.0

Answer: b
Explanation: Given : Initial point (5, 4), Final point (7, 2), Centre (5, 4)
So, the G, N codes for this motion are N010GO2X7.0Y2.0 15.0J2.0
where, GO2 ” Clockwise circular interpolation
X7.0Y2.0 ” Final point
I5.0J2.0 ” Centre point.

3. The tool of an NC machine has to move along a circular arc from (5, 5) to (10, 10) while performing an operation. The centre of the arc is at (10, 5). Which one of the following NC tool path command performs the above mentioned operation?
a) N010 GO2 X10 Y10 X5 Y5 R5
b) N010 GO3 X10 Y10 X5 Y5 R5
c) N010 GO1 X5 Y5 X10 Y10 R5
d) N010 GO2 X5 Y5 X10 Y10 R5

Answer: a
Explanation: N010 “represent start the operation
GO2 “represent circular (clock wise) interpolation
X10Y10 “represent final coordinates

X5Y5 “represent starting coordinate
R5 “represent radius of the arc
So, NC tool path command is, N010 GO2 X10 Y10 X5 Y5 R5.

4. NC contouring is an example of
a) continuous path positioning
b) point-to-point positioning
c) absolute positioning
d) incremental positioning

Answer: a
Explanation: NC contouring is a continuous path positioning system. Its function is to synchronize the axes of motion to generate a predetermined path, generally a line or a circular arc.

5. Match the following:

NC code	Definition
P. M05	1. Absolute coordinate system
Q. G01	2. Dwell
R. G04	3. Spindle stop
S. G09	4. Linear interpolation

a) P-2, Q-3, R-4, S-1
b) P-3, Q-4, R-1, S-2
c) P-3, Q-4, R-2, S-1
d) P-4, Q-3, R-2, S-1

Answer: c
Explanation: NC code Definition
P. M05 3. Spindle stop
Q. G01 4. Linear interpolation
R. G04 2. Dwell
S. G09 1. Absolute coordinate system
So, correct pairs are, P-3, Q-4, R-2, S-1.

6. In a CNC program block, N002 GO2 G91 X40 Z40……,GO2 and G91 refer to
a) circular interpolation in counterclockwise direction and incremental dimension
b) circular interpolation in counterclockwise direction and absolute dimension
c) circular interpolation in clockwise direction and incremental dimension

d) circular interpolation in clockwise direction and absolute dimension

Answer: c
Explanation: GO2 represent circular interpolation in clockwise direction.
G91 represent incremental dimension.

7. Numerical control ___________
a) applies only to milling machines
b) is a method for producing exact number of parts per hour
c) is a method for controlling by means of set of instructions
d) none of the mentioned

Answer: c
Explanation: NC is a method for controlling by means of set of instructions.
CNC performs the data processing functions.

8. Computer will perform the data processing functions in
a) NC
b) CNC
c) DNC
d) None of the mentioned

Answer: b
Explanation: NC is a method for controlling by means of set of instructions.
CNC performs the data processing functions.

9. Control loop unit of M.C.U is always
a) a hardware unit
b) a software unit
c) a control unit
d) none of the mentioned

Answer: a
Explanation: None.

10. The repeatability of NC machine depends on
a) control loop errors
b) mechanical errors
c) electrical errors

d) none of the mentioned

Answer: b
Explanation: None.

11. Rotation about Z-axis is called
a) a-axis
b) b-axis
c) c-axis
d) none of the mentioned

Answer: c
Explanation: Rotation about X-axis is called a-axis.
Rotation about Y-axis is called b-axis.
Rotation about Z-axis is called c-axis.

12. Rotation of spindle is designated by one of the following axis:
a) a-axis
b) b-axis
c) c-axis
d) none of the mentioned

Answer: d
Explanation: None.

13. The linking of computer with a communication system is called
a) networking
b) pairing
c) interlocking
d) assembling

Answer: a
Explanation: Networking is the practice of linking two or more computing devices together for the purpose of sharing data.
Pairing is the linking of computer with a communication system.
Interlocking is to fit into each other, as parts of machinery, so that all action is synchronized.

14. The process of putting data into a storage location is called
a) reading

b) writing
c) controlling
d) hand shaking

Answer: b
Explanation: Reading is the process of copying data from a memory location. Writing is the process of putting data into a storage location.

15. The process of copying data from a memory location is called
a) reading
b) writing
c) controlling
d) hand shaking

Answer: a
Explanation: Reading is the process of copying data from a memory location. Writing is the process of putting data into a storage location.

16. Designs are periodically modified to
a) improve product performance
b) strive for zero-based rejection and waste
c) make products easier and faster to manufacture
d) all of the mentioned

Answer: d
Explanation: Designs are periodically modified to
a) Improve product performance
b) Strive for zero-based rejection and waste
c) Make products easier and faster to manufacture
d) Consider new materials and processes that are continually being developed.

17. The expected qualities of a product are
a) it satisfies the needs and expectations of the customer
b) it has a pleasing appearance and handles well
c) it has high reliability and functions safely over its intended life
d) all of the mentioned

Answer: d
Explanation: Generally, however, a high-quality product is considered to have at least the following characteristics:
a) it satisfies the needs and expectations of the customer

b) it has a pleasing appearance and handles well
c) it has high reliability and functions safely over its intended life
d) it is compatible with and responsive to the customer's capabilities and working environment
e) installation, maintenance, and future improvements are easy to perform and at low cost.

18. The life cycle of a product includes
a) extraction of natural resources
b) processing of raw materials
c) manufacturing of products
d) all of the mentioned

Answer: d
Explanation: The life cycle involves consecutive and interlinked stages of a product or a service, from the very beginning to its disposal or recycling, and includes the following:
a) extraction of natural resources
b) processing of raw materials
c) manufacturing of products
d) transportation and distribution of the product to the customer
e) use, maintenance, and reuse of the product
f) recovery, recycling, and reuse of the components of the product.

19. Life-cycle engineering is also called
a) green design
b) expensive design
c) easy design
d) none of the mentioned

Answer: a
Explanation: The major aim of life-cycle engineering (LCE) is to consider reusing and recycling the components of a product, beginning with the earliest stage: product design. Life-cycle engineering is also called green design or green engineering.

20. Sustainable manufacturing is required for
a) conserving resources
b) proper maintenance
c) reuse
d) all of the mentioned

Answer: d
Explanation: The concept of sustainable manufacturing emphasizes the need for conserving resources, particularly through proper maintenance and reuse.

21. The mechanical properties of good product material are
a) strength
b) toughness
c) ductility
d) all of the mentioned

Answer: d
Explanation: Mechanical properties include strength, toughness, ductility, stiffness, hardness, and resistance to fatigue, creep, and impact.

22. The physical properties of good product material are
a) density
b) melting point
c) specific heat
d) all of the mentioned

Answer: d
Explanation: Physical properties include density, melting point, specific heat, thermal and electrical conductivity, thermal expansion, and magnetic properties.

23. The chemical properties of good product material are
a) oxidation
b) corrosion
c) surface treatment
d) all of the mentioned

Answer: d
Explanation: Chemical properties of primary concern in manufacturing are susceptibility to oxidation and corrosion and to the various surface-treatment processes.

24. Properties of workpiece materials are
a) geometric features of the part
b) production rate and quantity
c) process selection consideration
d) all of the mentioned

Answer: d
Explanation: None.

25. Considerations of costing systems are
a) life cycle costs
b) machine usage
c) cost of purchasing machinery
d) all of the mentioned

Answer: d
Explanation: Costing Systems, also called cost justification, typically include the following considerations: (a) intangible benefits of quality improvements and inventory reduction, (b) life-cycle costs, (c) machine usage, (d) cost of purchasing machinery compared with that of leasing it, (e) financial risks involved in implementing highly automated systems, and (f) new technologies and their impact on products.

26. Thickness of tooth measured along the pitch circle is known as
a) Tooth thickness
b) Backlash
c) Face width
d) Top land

Answer: a
Explanation: Tooth thickness is the thickness of tooth measured along the pitch circle.

27. Difference between space width and to thickness of tooth along the pitch circle is known as
a) Tooth thickness
b) Backlash
c) Face width
d) Top land

Answer: b
Explanation: Backlash is the Difference between space width and to thickness of tooth along the pitch circle.

28. Length of tooth parallel to gear axis is known as
a) Tooth thickness

b) Backlash
c) Face width
d) Top land

Answer: c
Explanation: Face width is the length of tooth parallel to gear axis.

29. Top surface of tooth is known as
a) Tooth thickness
b) Backlash
c) Face width
d) Top land

Answer: d
Explanation: Top land is the top surface of tooth.

30. Bottom surface of the tooth between two adjacent fillets is known as
a) Flank
b) Face
c) Bottom Land
d) Fillet

Answer: c
Explanation: Bottom surface of the tooth between two adjacent fillets is known as bottom land.

PRODUCTION PLANNING AND CONTROL

INIRODUCTION AND MEANING

Production planning and control is a tool available to the management to achieve the stated objectives. Thus, a production system is encompassed by the four factors. i.e., quantity, quality, cost and time. Production planning starts with the analysis of the given data, i.e., demand for products, delivery schedule etc., and on the basis of the information available, a scheme of utilisation of firm's resources like machines, materials and men are worked out to obtain the target in the most economical way.

Once the plan is prepared, then execution of plan is performed in line with the details given in the plan. Production control comes into action if there is any deviation between the actual and planned. The corrective action is taken so as to achieve the targets set as per plan by using control techniques.

Thus, production planning and control can be defined as the "direction and coordination of firms' resources towards attaining the prefixed goals." Production planning and control helps to achieve uninterrupted flow of materials through production line by making available the materials at right time and required quantity.

Need For Production Planning And Conirol

The present techno-economic scenario of India emphasizes on competitiveness in manufacturing. Indian industries have to streamline the production activities and attain the maximum utilisation of firms' resources to enhance the productivity. Production planning and control serves as a useful tool to coordinate the activities of the production system by proper planning and control system. Production system can be compared to the nervous system with PPC as a brain. Production planning and control is needed to achieve:

1. Effective utilisation of firms' resources.
2. To achieve the production objectives with respect to quality, quantity, cost and timeliness of delivery.
3. To obtain the uninterrupted production flow in order to meet customers varied demand with respect to quality and committed delivery schedule.

4. To help the company to supply good quality products to the customer on the continuous basis at competitive rates.
5. Production planning is a pre-production activity. It is the pre-determination of manufacturing requirements such as manpower, materials, machines and manufacturing process.

Ray wild defines "Production planning is the determination, acquisition and arrangement of all facilities necessary for future production of products." It represents the design of production system. Apart from planning the resources, it is going to organize the production.

Based on the estimated demand for company's products, it is going to establish the production programme to meet the targets set using the various resources.

Production Control

Inspite of planning to the minute details, most of the time it is not possible to achieve production 100 per cent as per the plan. There may be innumerable factors which affect the production system and because of which there is a deviation from the actual plan. Some of the factors that affect are:

1. Non-availability of materials (due to shortage, etc.);
2. Plant, equipment and machine breakdown;
3. Changes in demand and rush orders;
4. Absenteeism of workers; and
5. Lack of coordination and communication between various functional areas of business.

Thus, if there is a deviation between actual production and planned production, the control function comes into action. Production control through control mechanism tries to take corrective action to match the planned and actual production. Thus, production control reviews the progress of the work, and takes corrective steps in order to ensure that programmed production takes place. The essential steps in control activity are:

1. Initiating the production,
2. Progressing, and
3. Corrective action based upon the feedback and reporting back to the production planning.

Objectives of Production Planning and Control

Following are the objectives of production planning and control:

1. Systematic planning of production activities to achieve the highest efficiency in production of goods/services.
2. To organize the production facilities like machines, men, etc., to achieve stated production objectives with respect to quantity and quality time and cost.
3. Optimum scheduling of resources.
4. Coordinate with other departments relating to production to achieve regular balanced and uninterrupted production flow.
5. To conform to delivery commitments.
6. Materials planning and control.
7. To be able to make adjustments due to changes in demand and rush orders.

Phases Of Production Planning And Conirol

Production planning and control has three phases namely:

a) Planning Phase
b) Action Phase
c) Control Phase

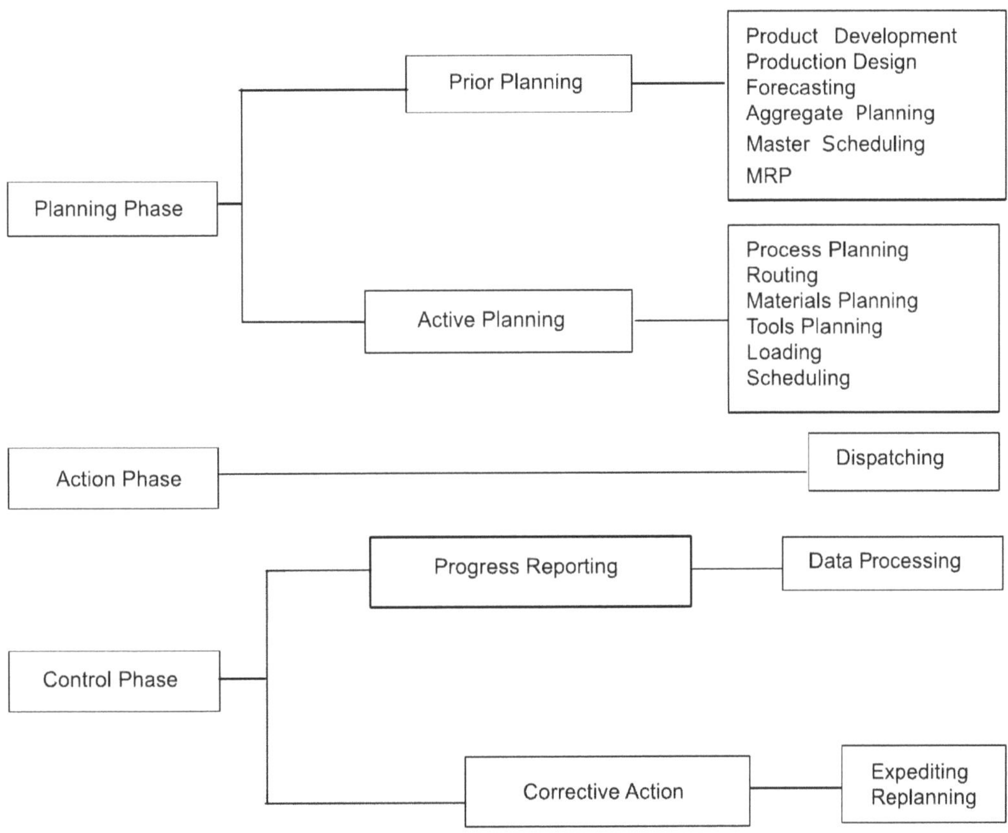

Fig. 5.1 Phases of production planning and control

Planning Phase

Planning is an exercise of intelligent anticipation in order to establish how an objective can be achieved or a need fulfilled in circumstances, which are invariably restrictive. Production planning determines the optimal schedule and sequence of operations economic batch quantity, machine assignment and dispatching priorities for sequencing.

It has two categories of planning namely.

1. Prior planning
2. Active planning.

Prior Planning

Prior planning means pre-production planning. This includes all the planning efforts, which are taking place prior to the active planning.

Modules of pre-planning

The modules of prior planning are as follows:

1. Product development and design is the process of developing a new product with all the features which are essential for effective use in the field, and designing it accordingly. At the design stage, one has to take several aspects of design like, design for selling, design for manufacturing and design for usage.
2. Forecasting is an estimate of demand, which will happen in future. Since, it is only an estimate based on the past demand, proper care must be taken while estimating it. Given the sales forecast, the factory capacity, the aggregate inventory levels and size of the work force, the manager must decide at what rate of production to operate the plant over an intermediate planning horizon.
3. Aggregate planning aims to find out a product wise planning over the intermediate planning horizon.
4. Material requirement planning is a technique for determining the quantity and timing for the acquisition of dependent items needed to satisfy the master production schedule.

Active Planning

The modules of active planning are: Process planning and routing, Materials planning. Tools planning, Loading, Scheduling etc.

1. Process planning and routing is a complete determination of the specific technological process steps and their sequence to produce products at the desired quality, quantity and cost. It determines the method of manufacturing a product selects the tools and equipments, analyses how the manufacturing of the product will fit into the facilities. Routing in particular prescribes the flow of work in the plant and it is related to the considerations of layout, temporary locations for raw materials and components and materials handling systems.
2. A material planning is a process which determines the requirements of various raw materials/subassemblies by considering the trade-off between various cost components like, carrying cost, ordering cost, shortage cost, and so forth. 3. Tools' planning determines the requirements of various tools by taking process specification (surface finish, length of the job, overall depth of cut etc.), material specifications (type of material used, hardness of the material, shape and size of the material etc.) and equipment specifications (speed range, feed range, depth of cut range etc.).

3. Loading is the process of assigning jobs to several machines such that there is a load balance among the machines. This is relatively a complex task, which can be managed with the help of efficient heuristic procedures.
4. Scheduling is the time phase of loading and determines when and in what sequence the work will be carried out. This fixes the starting as well as the finishing time for each job.

Action Phase

Action phase has the major step of dispatching. Dispatching is the transition from planning phase to action phase. In this phase, the worker is ordered to start manufacturing the product. The tasks which are included in dispatching are job order, store issue order, tool order, time ticket, inspection order, move order etc.

The job order number is the key item which is to be mentioned in all other reports/orders. Stores issue order gives instruction to stores to issue materials for manufacturing the product as per product specifications. As per tooling requirements for manufacturing the product, the tool order instruct the tool room to issue necessary tools. Time ticket is nothing but a card which is designed to note down the actual time taken at various processes. This information is used for deciding the costs for future jobs of similar nature and also for performing variance analysis, which helps to exercise control.

Job order is the official authorization to the shop floor to start manufacturing the product. Generally, the process sequence will contain some testing and inspection. So, these are to be instructed to inspection wing in the form of inspection order for timely testing and inspection so that the amount of rework is minimized. The manufacture of product involves moving raw materials/subassemblies to the main line. This is done by a well-designed materials handling system. So, proper instruction is given to the materials handling facilities for major movements of materials/subassemblies in the form of a move order. Movements which involve less distance and fewer loads are managed at the shop floor level based on requests from operators.

Control Phase

The control phase has the following two major modules:

1. Progress reporting, and
2. Corrective action.

Progress Reporting

In progress reporting, the data regarding what is happening with the job is collected. Also, it helps to make comparison with the present level of performance. The various data pertaining to materials rejection, process variations, equipment failures, operator efficiency, operator absenteeism, tool life, etc., are collected and analyzed for the purpose of progress reporting. These data are used for performing variance analysis, which would help us to identify critical areas that deserve immediate attention for corrective actions.

Corrective Action

The tasks under corrective action primarily make provisions for an unexpected event. Some examples of corrective actions are creating schedule flexibility, schedule modifications, capacity modifications, make or buy decisions, expediting the work, pre-planning, and so on. Due to unforeseen reasons such as, machine breakdown, labour absenteeism, too much rejection due to poor material quality etc., it may not be possible to realize the schedule as per the plan. Under such condition, it is better to reschedule the whole product mix so that we get a clear picture of the situation to progress further. Under such situation, it is to be re-examined for selecting appropriate course of action. Expediting means taking action if the progress reporting indicates deviations from the originally set targets. Pre-planning of the whole affair becomes essential in case the expediting fails to bring the deviated plan to its right path.

Functions Of Producton Planning And Conirol

Functions of production planning and controlling is classified into:

1. Pre-planning fuction
2. Planning function
3. Control function

The functions of production planning and controlling are depicted in the Fig. 5.2.

Pre-PlanNing Function

Pre-planning is a macro level planning and deals with analysis of data and is an outline of the planning policy based upon the forecasted demand, market analysis and product design and

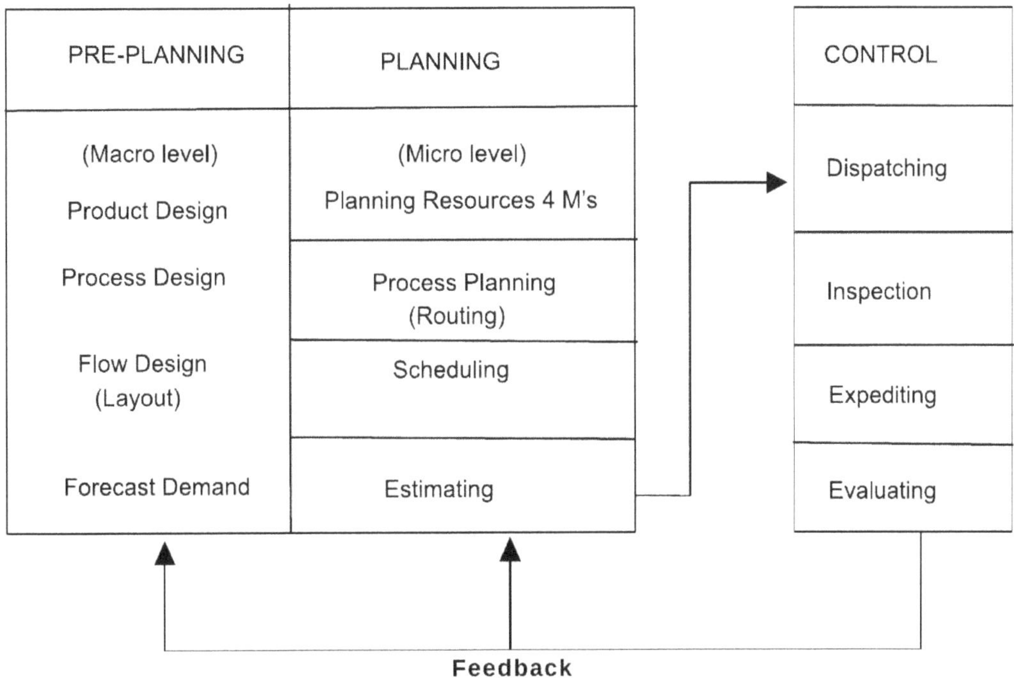

Fig. 5.2 Functions of production planning and control development. This stage is concerned with process design (new processes and developments, equipment policy and replacement and workflow (Plant layout). The pre-planning function of PPC is concerned with decision-making with respect to methods, machines and workflow with respect to availability, scope and capacity.

Planning Function

The planning function starts once the task to be accomplished is specified, with the analysis of four M's, i.e., Machines, Methods, Materials and Manpower. This is followed by process planning (routing). Both short-term (near future) and long-term planning are considered. Standardisation, simplification of products and processes are given due consideration.

Control Function

Control phase is affected by dispatching, inspection and expediting materials control, analysis of work-in-process. Finally, evaluation makes the PPC cycle complete and corrective actions are taken through feedback from analysis. A good communication, and feedback system is essential to enhance and ensure effectiveness of PPC.

Parameters for PPC

The functions of PPC can be explained with the following parameters:

1. Materials: Raw materials, finished parts and bought out components should be made available in required quantities and at required time to ensure the correct start and end for each operation resulting in uninterrupted production. The function includes the specification of materials (quality and quantity) delivery dates, variety reduction (standardisation) procurement and make or buy decisions.
2. Machines and equipment: This function is related with the detailed analysis of available production facilities, equipment down time, maintenance policy procedure and schedules. Concerned with economy of jigs and fixtures, equipment availability. Thus, the duties include the analysis of facilities and making their availability with minimum down time because of breakdowns.
3. Methods: This function is concerned with the analysis of alternatives and selection of the best method with due consideration to constraints imposed. Developing specifications for processes is an important aspect of PPC and determination of sequence of operations.
4. Process planning (Routing): It is concerned with selection of path or route which the raw material should follow to get transformed into finished product. The duties include:
   a) Fixation of path of travel giving due consideration to layout.
   b) Breaking down of operations to define each operation in detail.
   c) Deciding the set-up time and process time for each operation.

5 **Estimating:** Once the overall method and sequence of operations is fixed and process sheet for each operation is available, then the operations times are estimated. This function is carried out using extensive analysis of operations along with methods and routing and a standard time for operation are established using work measurement techniques.

6 **Loading and scheduling:** Scheduling is concerned with preparation of machine loads and fixation of starting and completion dates for each of the operations. Machines have to be loaded according to their capability of performing the given task and according to their capacity. Thus, the duties include:

   a) Loading, the machines as per their capability and capacity.
   b) Determining the start and completion times for each operation.
   c) To coordinate with sales department regarding delivery schedules.

7 **Dispatching:** This is the execution phase of planning. It is the process of setting production activities in motion through release of orders and instructions. It authorises

the start of production activities by releasing materials, components, tools, fixtures and instruction sheets to the operator. The activities involved are:

a) To assign definite work to definite machines, work centres and men.
b) To issue required materials from stores.
c) To issue jigs, fixtures and make them available at correct point of use.
d) Release necessary work orders, time tickets, etc., to authorise timely start of operations.
e) To record start and finish time of each job on each machine or by each man.

8 **Expediting:** This is the control tool that keeps a close observation on the progress of the work. It is logical step after dispatching which is called 'follow-up'. It coordinates extensively to execute the production plan. Progressing function can be divided into three parts, i.e., follow up of materials, follow up of work-in-process and follow up of assembly. The duties include:

a) Identification of bottlenecks and delays and interruptions because of which the production schedule may be disrupted.
b) To devise action plans (remedies) for correcting the errors.
c) To see that production rate is in line with schedule.

9 **Inspection:** It is a major control tool. Though the aspects of quality control are the separate function, this is of very much important to PPC both for the execution of the current plans and its scope for future planning. This forms the basis for knowing the limitations with respects to methods, processes, etc., which is very much useful for evaluation phase.

10 **Evaluation:** This stage though neglected is a crucial to the improvement of productive efficiency. A thorough analysis of all the factors influencing the production planning and control helps to identify the weak spots and the corrective action with respect to pre-planning and planning will be affected by feedback. The success of this step depends on the communication, data and information gathering and analysis.

Operations Planning and Scheduung Sysiems

Operations planning and scheduling systems concern with the volume and timing of outputs, the utilisation of operations capacity at desired levels for competitive effectiveness. These systems must fit together activities at various levels, form top to bottom, in support of one another, as shown in Fig. 5.3. Note that the time orientation ranges from long to short as we progress from top to bottom in the hierarchy. Also, the level of detail in the planning process ranges from broad at the top to detail at the bottom.

Components of Operations Planning and Scheduling System

The Business Plan

The business plan is a statement of the organization's overall level of business activity for the coming six to eighteen months, usually expressed in terms of outputs (in volume of sales) for its various product groups, a set of individual products that share or consume common blocks of capacity in the manufacturing process. It also specifies the overall inventory and backlog levels that will be maintained during the planning period. The business plan is an agreement between all functional areas-finance, production, marketing, engineering, R & D-about the level of activity and the products they are committed to support. The business plan is not concerned with all the details and specific timing of the actions for executing the plan. Instead, it determines a feasible general posture for competing to achieve its major goals. The resulting plan guides the lower-level, more details decisions.

Aggregate Production (Output) Planning

The process of determining output levels of product groups over the coming six to eighteen months on a weekly or monthly basis. It identifies the overall level of outputs in support of the business plan. The plan recognizes the division's existing fixed capacity and the company's overall policies for maintaining inventories and backlogs, employment stability and subcontracting.

Aggregate Capacity Planning

It is the process of testing the feasibility of aggregate output plans and evaluating overall capacity utilisation. A statement of desired output is useful only if it is feasible. Thus, it addresses the supply side of the firm's ability to meet the demand. As for aggregate output plans, each plant, facility, or division requires its own aggregate capacity plan. Capacity and output must be in balance, as indicated by the arrow between them in Fig. 5.3. A capacity plan translates an output plan into input terms, approximating how much of the division's capacity will be consumed. Although these basic capacities are fixed, management can manipulate the short-term capacities by the ways they deploy their work force, by subcontracting, or by using multiple work shifts to adjust the timing of overall outputs. As a result, the aggregate planning process balances output levels, capacity constraints, and temporary capacity adjustments to meet demand and utilise capacity at desired levels during the coming months. The resulting plan sets limits on the master production schedule.

Master Production Scheduling (MPS)

MPS is a schedule showing week by week how many of each product must be produced according to customer orders and demand forecasts. Its purpose is to meet the demand for individual products in the product group. This more detailed level of planning disaggregates the product groups into individual products and indicates when they will be produced. The MPS is an important link between marketing and production. It shows when incoming sales orders can be scheduled into production, and when each shipment can be scheduled for delivery. It also takes into account current backlogs so that production and delivery schedules are realistic.

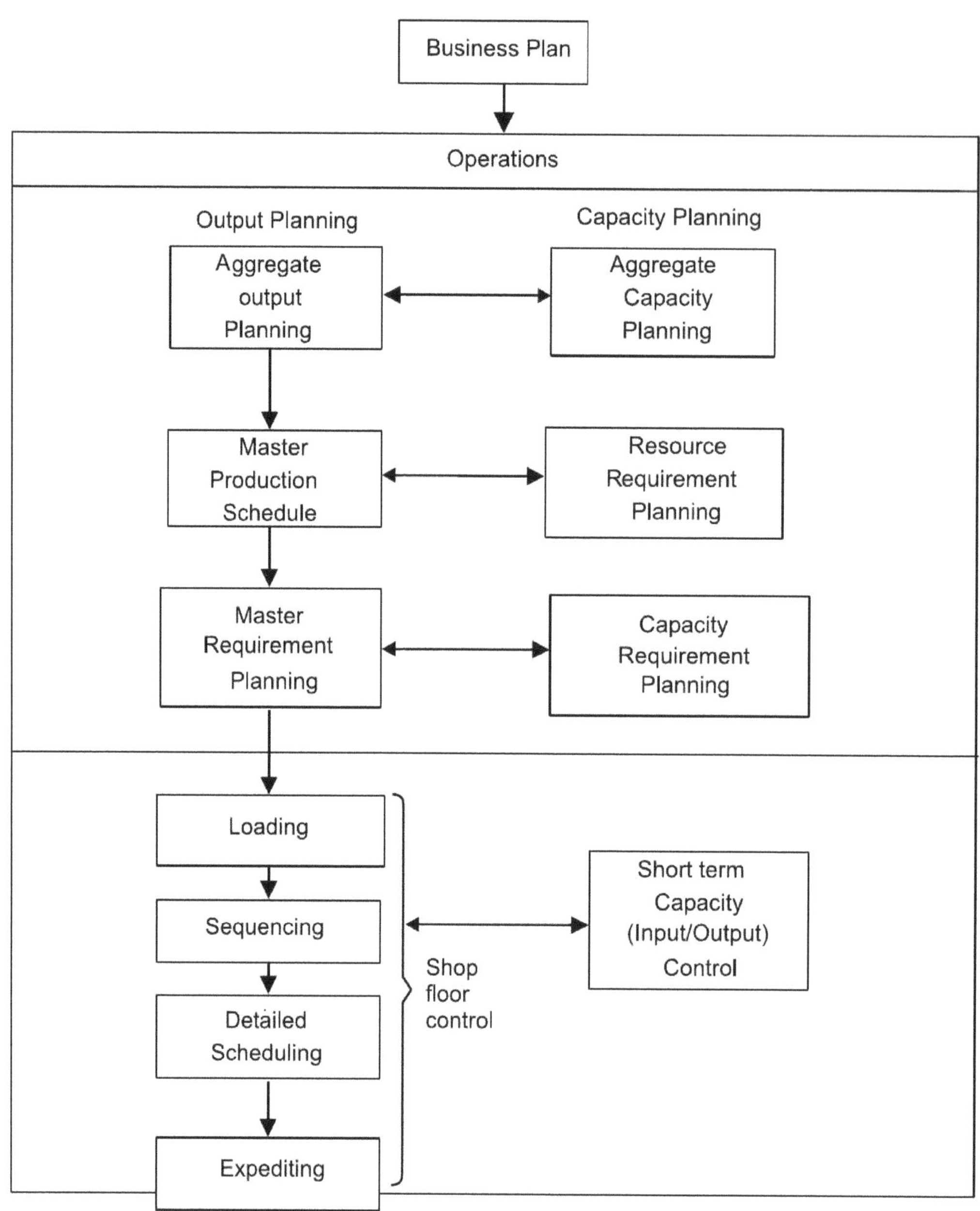

Fig. 5.3 Operations planning and scheduling system.

Resource Requirement Planning

Resource requirement planning (rough-cut capacity planning) is the process of testing the feasibility of master production schedule in terms of capacity. This step ensures that a proposed MPS does not inadvertently overload any key department, work centre, or machine, making the MPS unworkable.

Material Requirement PlanNing

Material requirement planning (MRP) is a system of planning and scheduling the time phased material requirements for releasing materials and receiving materials that enable the master production schedule to be implemented. Thus, the master production schedule is the driving force for material requirements planning. MRP provides information such as due dates for components that are subsequently used for shop floor control. Once this information is available, it enables managers to estimate the detailed requirements for each work centres.

Capacity Requirement Planning

Capacity requirement planning (CRP) is an iterative process of modifying the MPS or planned resources to make capacity consistent with the production schedule. CRP is a companion process used with MRP to identify in detail the capacity required to execute the material requirement planning. At this level, more accurate comparisons of available and needed capacity for scheduled workloads are possible.

Shop Floor Control

Shop floor control involves the activities that execute and control shop operations namely loading, sequencing, detailed scheduling and expediting jobs in production. It coordinates the weekly and daily activities that get jobs done. Individual jobs are assigned to machines and work centres (loading), the sequence of processing the jobs for priority control is determined, start times and job assignments for each stage of processing are decided (detailed scheduling) and materials and work flows from station to station are monitored and adjusted (expediting).

Loading

Each job (customer order) may have its unique product specification and, hence, it is unique through various work centres in the facility. As new job orders are released, they are assigned or allocated among the work centres, thus establishing how much of a load each work centre must carry during the coming planning period. This assignment is known as loading (sometimes called shop loading as machine loading).

Sequencing

This stage establishes the priorities for jobs in the queues (waiting lines) at the work centres. Priority sequencing specifies the order in which the waiting jobs are processed; it requires the adoption of a priority sequencing rule.

Detailed Scheduling

Detailed scheduling determines start times, finish times and work assignments for all jobs at each work centre. Calendar times are specified when job orders, employees, and materials (inputs), as well as job completion (outputs), should occur at each work centre. By estimating how long each job will take to complete and when it is due, schedulers can establish start and finish dates and develop the detailed schedule.

Expediting

Expediting is a process of tracking a job's progress and taking special actions to move it through the facility. In tracking a job's progress, special action may be needed to keep the job moving through the facility on time. Manufacturing or service operations disruptions-equipments breakdowns, unavailable materials, last-minute priority changes, require managers to deviate from plans and schedules and expedite an important job on a special handling basis.

Input/Output Control

Input/output control related to the activities to monitor actual versus planned utilisation of a work centre's capacity. Output plans and schedules call for certain levels of capacity at a work centre, but actual utilisation may differ from what was planned. Actual versus planned utilisation of the work centre's capacity can be monitored by using input-output reports and, when discrepancies exist, adjustments can be made. The important components of operations planning and scheduling system has been explained in detail in the following paragraphs.

Aggregate Planning

Aggregate planning is an intermediate term planning decision. It is the process of planning the quantity and timing of output over the intermediate time horizon (3 months to one year). Within this range, the physical facilities are assumed to -10 be fixed for the planning period. Therefore, fluctuations in demand must be met by varying labour and inventory schedule. Aggregate planning seeks the best combination to minimise costs.

Aggregate Planning Stategies

The variables of the production system are labour, materials and capital. More labour effort is required to generate higher volume of output. Hence, the employment and use of overtime (OT) are the two relevant variables. Materials help to regulate output. The alternatives available to the company are inventories, back ordering or subcontracting of items.

These controllable variables constitute pure strategies by which fluctuations in demand and uncertainties in production activities can be accommodated by using the following steps:

1. Vary the size or the workforce: Output is controlled by hiring or laying off workers in proportion to changes in demand.
2. Vary the hours worked: Maintain the stable workforce but permit idle time when there is a slack and permit overtime (OT) when demand is peak.
3. Vary inventory levels: Demand fluctuations can be met by large amount of inventory.
4. Subcontract: Upward shift in demand from low level. Constant production rates can be met by using subcontractors to provide extra capacity.

Aggregate Planning Guidelines

The following are the guidelines for aggregate planning:

1. Determine corporate policy regarding controllable variables.
2. Use a good forecast as a basis for planning.
3. Plan in proper units of capacity.
4. Maintain the stable workforce.
5. Maintain needed control over inventories.
6. Maintain flexibility to change.
7. Respond to demand in a controlled manner.
8. Evaluate planning on a regular base.

Master Production Schedule (Mps)

Master scheduling follows aggregate planning. It expresses the overall plans in terms of specific end items or models that can be assigned priorities. It is useful to plan for the material and capacity requirements.

Flowchart of aggregate plan and master production schedule is shown in Fig. 5.4

Time interval used in master scheduling depends upon the type, volume, and component lead times of the products being produced. Normally weekly time intervals are used. The time horizon covered by the master schedule also depends upon product characteristics and lead times. Some master schedules cover a period as short as few weeks and for some products it is more than a year.

Functions of MPS

Master Production Schedule (MPS) gives a formal detail of the production plan and converts this plan into specific material and capacity requirements. The requirements with respect to labour, material and equipment is then assessed.

The main functions of MPS are:

1 To translate aggregate plans into specific end items: Aggregate plan determines level of operations that tentatively balances the market demands with the material, labour and equipment capabilities of the company. A master schedule translates this plan into specific number of end items to be produced in specific time period.

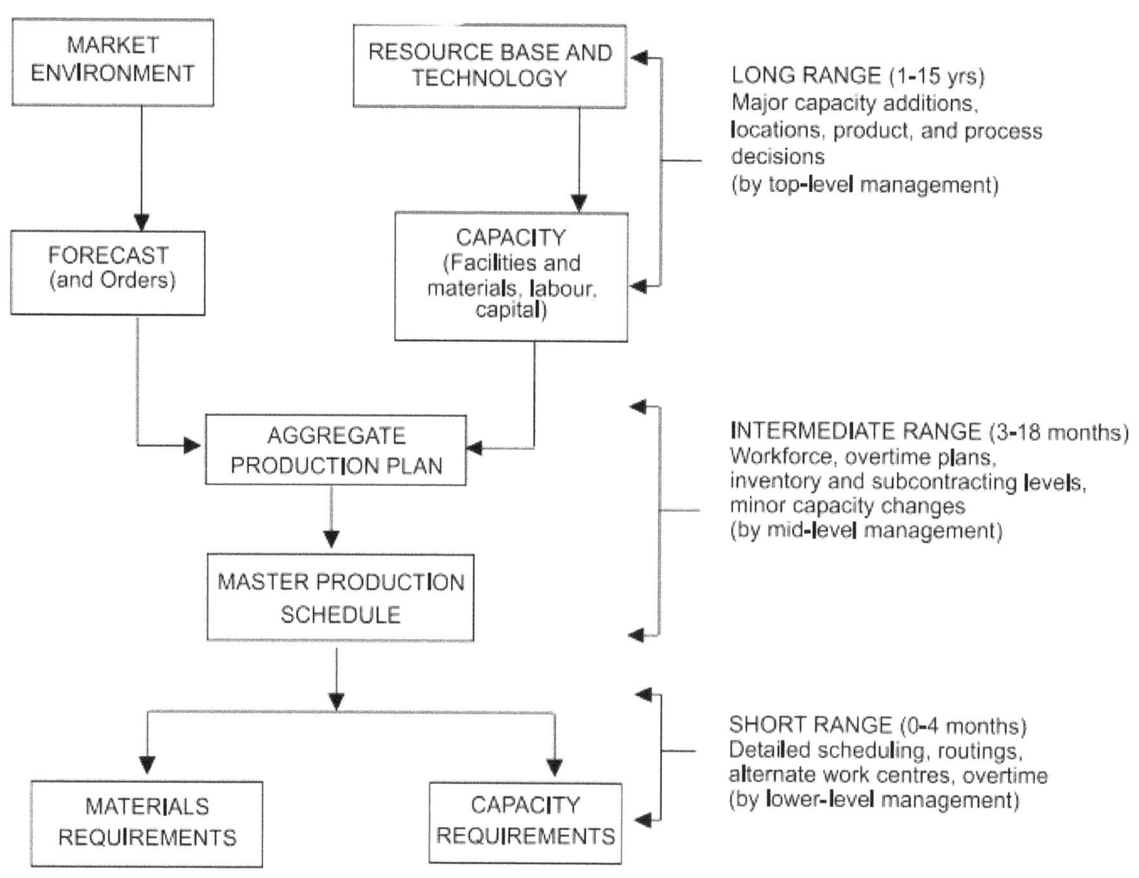

Fig. 5.4 Flowchart of aggregate plan and master schedule

2. Evaluate alternative schedules: Master schedule is prepared by trial and error. Many computer simulation models are available to evaluate the alternate schedules.

3. Generate material requirement: It forms the basic input for material requirement planning (MRP).

4. Generate capacity requirements: Capacity requirements are directly derived from MPS. Master scheduling is thus a prerequisite for capacity planning.

5. Facilitate information processing: By controlling the load on the plant. Master schedule determines when the delivery should be made. It coordinates with other management information systems such as, marketing, finance, and personnel.

6. Effective utilization of capacity: By specifying end item requirements schedule establishes the load and utilization requirements for machines and equipment.

Material Requirement Planning (Mrp)

MRP refers to the basic calculations used to determine components required from end item requirements. It also refers to a broader information system that uses the dependence relationship to plan and control manufacturing operations.

"Materials Requirement Planning (MRP) is a technique for determining the quantity and timing for the acquisition of dependent demand items needed to satisfy master production schedule requirements."

Objectives of MRP

1. Inventory reduction: MRP determines how many components are required when they are required in order to meet the master schedule. It helps to procure the materials/ components as and when needed and thus avoid excessive build up of inventory.
2. Reduction in the manufacturing and delivery lead times: MRP identifies materials and component quantities, timings when they are needed, availabilities and procurements and actions required to meet delivery deadlines. MRP helps to avoid delays in production and priorities production activities by putting due dates on customer job order.
3. Realistic delivery commitments: By using MRP, production can give marketing timely information about likely delivery times to prospective customers.

4. Increased efficiency: MRP provides a close coordination among various work centres and hence help to achieve uninterrupted flow of materials through the production line. This increases the efficiency of production system.

MRP System

The inputs to the MRP system are: (1) A master production schedule, (2) An inventory status file and (3) Bill of materials (BOM).

Using these three information sources, the MRP processing logic (computer programme) provides three kinds of information (output) for each product component: order release requirements, order rescheduling and planned orders.

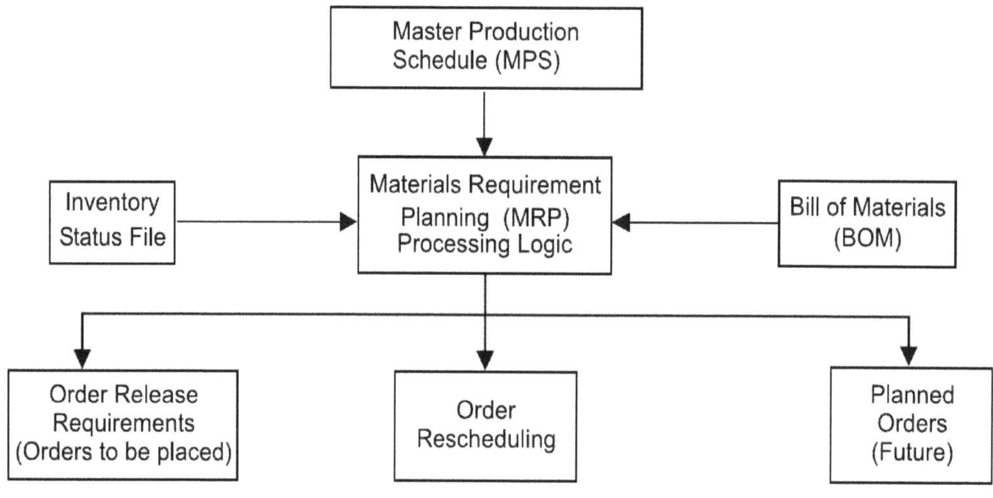

Fig. 5.5 MRP system

Master Production Schedule (MPS)

MPS is a series of time phased quantities for each item that a company produces, indicating how many are to be produced and when. MPS is initially developed from firm customer orders or from forecasts of demand before MRP system begins to operate. The MRP system whatever the master schedule demands and translates MPS end items into specific component requirements. Many systems make a simulated trial run to determine whether the proposed master can be satisfied.

Inventory Status File

Every inventory item being planned must have an inventory status file which gives complete and up to date information on the on-hand quantities, gross requirements, scheduled receipts and planned order releases for an item. It also includes planning information such as lot sizes, lead times, safety stock levels and scrap allowances.

Bill of MATERIALS (BOM)

BOM identifies how each end product is manufactured, specifying all subcomponents items, their sequence of build up, their quantity in each finished unit and the work centres performing the build up sequence. This information is obtained from product design documents, workflow analysis and other standard manufacturing information.

Capacity Planning

Design of the production system involves planning for the inputs, conversion process and outputs of production operation. The effective management of capacity is the most important responsibility of production management. The objective of capacity management (i.e., planning and control of capacity) is to match the level of operations to the level of demand.

Capacity planning is to be carried out keeping in mind future growth and expansion plans, market trends, sales forecasting, etc. It is a simple task to plan the capacity in case of stable demand. But in practice the demand will be seldom stable. The fluctuation of demand creates problems regarding the procurement of resources to meet the customer demand. Capacity decisions are strategic in nature. Capacity is the rate of productive capability of a facility. Capacity is usually expressed as volume of output per period of time.

Production managers are more concerned about the capacity for the following reasons:

- Sufficient capacity is required to meet the customers demand in time.
- Capacity affects the cost efficiency of operations.
- Capacity affects the scheduling system.
- Capacity creation requires an investment.
- Capacity planning is the first step when an organization decides to produce more or new products.

Measurement of Capacity Planning

The capacity of the manufacturing unit can be expressed in number of units of output per period. In some situations, measuring capacity is more complicated when they manufacture multiple products. In such situations, the capacity is expressed as man-hours or machine hours. The relationship between capacity and output is shown in Fig. 5.6.

1 Design capacity: Designed capacity of a facility is the planned or engineered rate of output of goods or services under normal or full-scale operating conditions.

  For example, the designed capacity of the cement plant is 100 TPD (Tonnes per day). Capacity of the sugar factory is 150 tonnes of sugarcane crushing per day.

2 System capacity: System capacity is the maximum output of the specific product or product mix the system of workers and machines is capable of producing as an integrated whole. System capacity is less than design capacity or at the most equal, because of the limitation of product mix, quality specification, breakdowns. The actual is even less because of many factors affecting the output such as actual demand, downtime due to machine/equipment failure, unauthorised absenteeism.

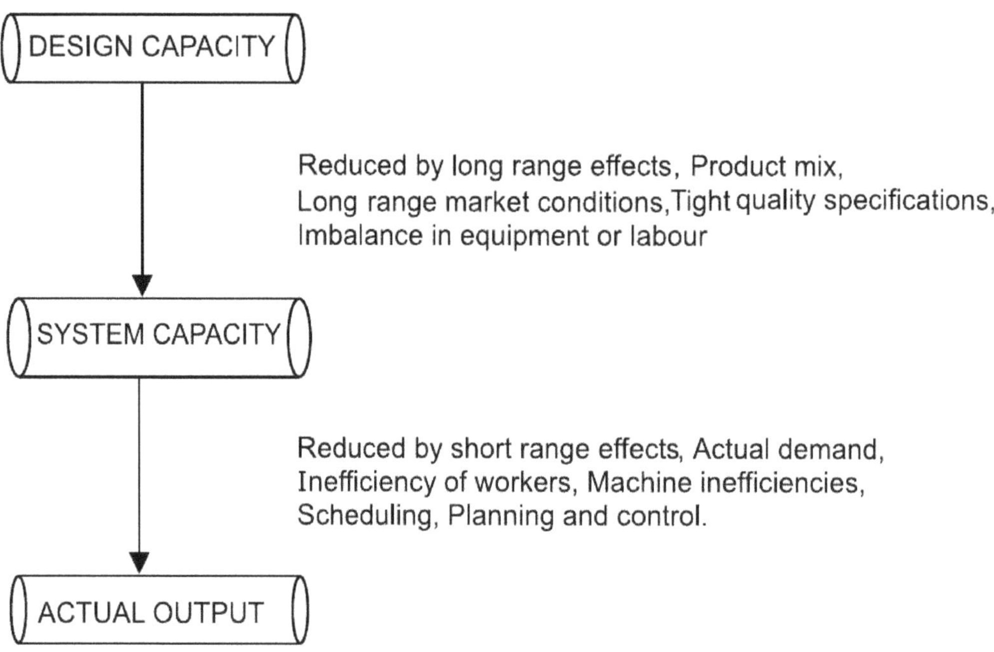

Fig. 5.6 Capacity and output relationship

The system capacity is less than design capacity because of long range uncontrollable factors. The actual output is still reduced because of short-term effects such as, breakdown of equipment, inefficiency of labour. The system efficiency is expressed as ratio of actual measured output to the system capacity.

$$\text{System Efficiency (SE)} = \frac{\text{Actual output}}{\text{System capacity}}$$

3 **Licensed capacity:** Capacity licensed by the various regulatory agencies or government authorities. This is the limitation on the output exercised by the government.

4 **Installed capacity:** The capacity provided at the time of installation of the plant is called installed capacity.

5 **Rated capacity:** Capacity based on the highest production rate established by actual trials is referred to as rated capacity.

Process of Capacity Planning

Capacity planning is concerned with defining the long-term and the short-term capacity needs of an organization and determining how those needs will be satisfied. Capacity planning decisions are taken based upon the consumer demand, and this is merged with the human, material and financial resources of the organization.

Capacity requirements can be evaluated from two perspectives-long-term capacity strategies and short-term capacity strategies.

Long-Term Capacity Strategies

Long-term capacity requirements are more difficult to determine because the future demand and technology are uncertain. Forecasting for five or ten years into the future is riskier and more difficult. Even sometimes company's today's products may not be existing in the future. Long range capacity requirements are dependent on marketing plans, product development and lifecycle of the product. Long-term capacity planning is concerned with accommodating major changes that affect overall level of the output in long-term. Marketing environmental assessment and implementing the long-term capacity plans in a systematic manner are the major responsibilities of management. Following parameters will affect long range capacity decisions.

1 Multiple products: Company's produce more than one product using the same facilities in order to increase the profit. The manufacturing of multiple products will reduce the risk of failure. Having more than one product helps the capacity planners to do a better job. Because products are in different stages of their life-cycles, it is easy to schedule them to get maximum capacity utilisation.

2 Phasing in capacity: In high technology industries, and in industries where technology developments are very fast, the rate of obsolescence is high. The products should be brought into the market quickly. The time to construct the facilities will be long and

there is no much time as the products should be introduced into the market quickly. Here the solution is phase in capacity on modular basis. Some commitment is made for building funds and men towards facilities over a period of 3-5 years. This is an effective way of capitalising on technological breakthroughs.

3 Phasing out capacity: The outdated manufacturing facilities cause excessive plant closures and down time. The impact of closures is not limited to only fixed costs of plant and machinery. Thus, the phasing out here is done with humanistic way without affecting the community. The phasing out options makes alternative arrangements for men like shifting them to other jobs or to other locations, compensating the employees, etc.

Short-Term Capacity Strategies

Managers often use forecasts of product demand to estimate the short-term workload the facility must handle. Managers looking ahead up to 12 months, anticipate output requirements for different products, and services. Managers then compare requirements with existing capacity and then take decisions as to when the capacity adjustments are needed.

For short-term periods of up to one-year, fundamental capacity is fixed. Major facilities will not be changed. Many short-term adjustments for increasing or decreasing capacity are possible. The adjustments to be required depend upon the conversion process like whether it is capital intensive or labour intensive or whether product can be stored as inventory.

Capital intensive processes depend on physical facilities, plant and equipment. Short-term capacity can be modified by operating these facilities more or less intensively than normal. In labour intensive processes short-term capacity can be changed by laying off or hiring people or by giving overtime to workers. The strategies for changing capacity also depend upon how long the product can be stored as inventory.

The short-term capacity strategies are:

1 Inventories: Stock of finished goods during slack periods to meet the demand during peak period.

2 Backlog: During peak periods, the willing customers are requested to wait and their orders are fulfilled after a peak demand period.

3 Employment level (hiring or firing): Hire additional employees during peak demand period and layoff employees as demand decreases.

4 Employee training: Develop multi-skilled employees through training so that they can be rotated among different jobs. The multi-skilling helps as an alternative to hiring employees.

5 Subcontracting: During peak periods, hire the capacity of other firms temporarily to make the component parts or products.

6 Process design: Change job contents by redesigning the job.

Rouing

Routing may be defined as the selection of path which each part of the product will follow while being transformed from raw materials to finished products. Path of the product will also give sequence of operation to be adopted while being manufactured.

In other way, routing means determination of most advantageous path to be followed from department to department and machine to machine till raw material gets its final shape, which involves the following steps:

a) Type of work to be done on product or its parts.
b) Operation required to do the work.
c) Sequence of operation required.
d) Where the work will be done.
e) A proper classification about the personnel required and the machine for doing the work.

For effective production control of a well-managed industry with standard conditions, the routing plays an important role, i.e., to have the best results obtained from available plant capacity. Thus, routing provides the basis for scheduling, dispatching and follow-up.

Techniques of Routing

While converting raw material into required goods different operations are to be performed and the selection of a particular path of operations for each piece is termed as 'Routing'. This selection of a particular path, i.e. sequence of operations must be the best and cheapest to have the lowest cost of the final product. The various routing techniques are:

1 Route card: This card always accompanies with the job throughout all operations. This indicates the material used during manufacturing and their progress from one operation to another. In addition to this the details of scrap and good work produced are also recorded.

2 **Work sheet:** It contains.

a) Specifications to be followed while manufacturing.
b) Instructions regarding routing of every part with identification number of machines and workplace of operation.

This sheet is made for manufacturing as well as for maintenance.

3 **Route sheet:** It deals with specific production order. Generally made from operation sheets. One sheet is required for each part or component of the order. These includes the following:

- o Number and other identification of order.
- o Symbol and identification of part.
- o Number of pieces to be made.
- o Number of pieces in each lot-if put through in lots.
- o Operation data which includes:
- o List of operation on the part.
- o Department in which operations are to be performed.
- o Machine to be used for each operation.
- o Fixed sequence of operation, if any.
- o Rate at which job must be completed, determined from the operation sheet.

4 Move order: Though this is document needed for production control, it is never used for routing system. Move order is prepared for each operation as per operation sheet. On this the quantity passed forward, scrapped and to be rectified are recorded. It is returned to planning office when the operation is completed.

Scheduling

Scheduling can be defined as "prescribing of when and where each operation necessary to manufacture the product is to be performed."

It is also defined as "establishing of times at which to begin and complete each event or operation comprising a procedure". The principle aim of scheduling is to plan the sequence of work so that production can be systematically arranged towards the end of completion of all products by due date.

Principles of Scheduling

1 The principle of optimum task size: Scheduling tends to achieve maximum efficiency when the task sizes are small, and all tasks of same order of magnitude.

2 Principle of optimum production plan: The planning should be such that it imposes an equal load on all plants.

3 Principle of optimum sequence: Scheduling tends to achieve the maximum efficiency when the work is planned so that work hours are normally used in the same sequence.

Inputs to Scheduling

1 Performance standards: The information regarding the performance standards (standard times for operations) helps to know the capacity in order to assign required machine hours to the facility.

2 Units in which loading and scheduling is to be expressed.

3 Effective capacity of the work centre.

4 Demand pattern and extent of flexibility to be provided for rush orders.

5 Overlapping of operations.

6 Individual job schedules.

Scheduling Stategies

Scheduling strategies vary widely among firms and range from 'no scheduling' to very sophisticated approaches.

These strategies are grouped into four classes:

1 Detailed scheduling: Detailed scheduling for specific jobs that are arrived from customers is impracticable in actual manufacturing situation. Changes in orders, equipment breakdown, and unforeseen events deviate the plans.

2 Cumulative scheduling: Cumulative scheduling of total workload is useful especially for long range planning of capacity needs. This may load the current period excessively and under load future periods. It has some means to control the jobs.

3 Cumulative detailed: Cumulative detailed combination is both feasible and practical approach. If master schedule has fixed and flexible portions.

4 Priority decision rules: Priority decision rules are scheduling guides that are used independently and in conjunction with one of the above strategies, i.e., first come first serve. These are useful in reducing Work-In-Process (WIP) inventory.

Types of Scheduling

Types of scheduling can be categorized as forward scheduling and backward scheduling.

1 Forward scheduling is commonly used in job shops where customers place their orders on "needed as soon as possible" basis. Forward scheduling determines start and finish times of next priority job by assigning it the earliest available time slot and from that time, determines when the job will be finished in that work centre. Since the job and its components start as early as possible, they will typically be completed before they are due at the subsequent work centres in the routing. The forward method generates in the process inventory that are needed at subsequent work centres and higher inventory cost. Forward scheduling is simple to use, and it gets jobs done in shorter lead times, compared to backward scheduling.

2 Backward scheduling is often used in assembly type industries and commit in advance to specific delivery dates. Backward scheduling determines the start and finish times for waiting jobs by assigning them to the latest available time slot that will enable each job to be completed just when it is due but done before. By assigning jobs as late as possible, backward scheduling minimizes inventories since a job is not completed until it must go directly to the next work centre on its routing. Forward and backward scheduling methods are shown in Fig. 5.7.

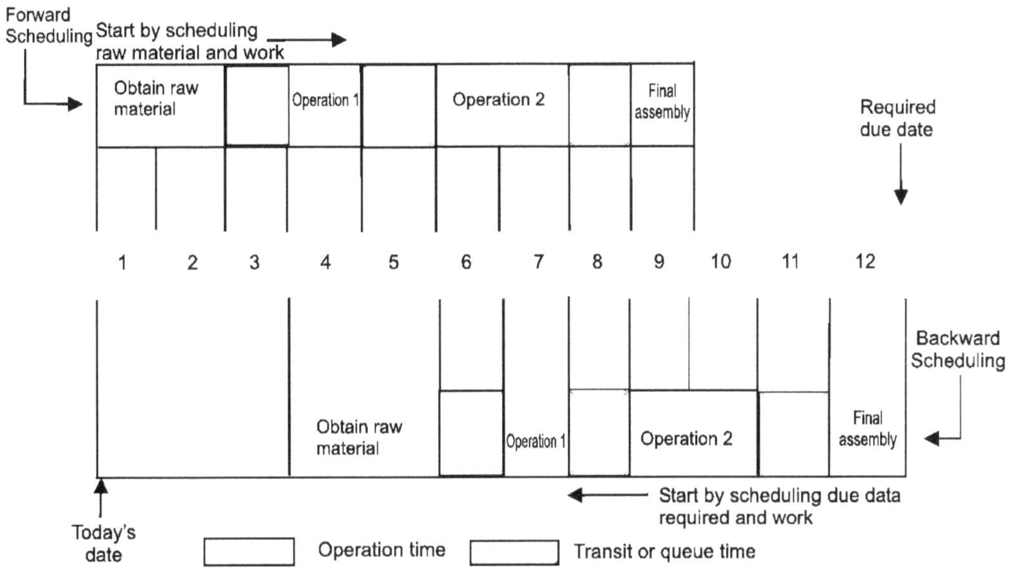

Fig. 5.7 Forward and backward scheduling

Scheduung Methodology

The scheduling methodology depends upon the type of industry, organization, product, and level of sophistication required. They are:

1 Charts and boards,

2 Priority decision rules, and

3 Mathematical programming methods.

Gantt Charts and Boards

Gantt charts and associated scheduling boards have been extensively used scheduling devices in the past, although many of the charts are now drawn by computer. Gantt charts are extremely easy to understand and can quickly reveal the current or planned situation to all concerned. They are used in several forms, namely,

(a) Scheduling or progress charts, which depicts the sequential schedule.

(b) Load charts, which show the work assigned to a group of workers or machines; and

(c) Record a chart, which are used to record the actual operating times and delays of workers and machines.

Priority Decision Rules

Priority decision rules are simplified guidelines for determining the sequence in which jobs will be done. In some firms these rules take the place of priority planning systems such as MRP systems. Following are some of the priority rules followed.

Symbol	Priority rule
FCFS	First come, first served
EDO	Earliest due date
LS	Least slack (that is, time due less processing time)
SPT	Shortest processing time
LPT	Longest processing time
PCO	Preferred customer order
RS	Random selection

Mathematical Programming Methods

Scheduling is a complex resource allocation problem. Firms process capacity, labour skills, materials and they seek to allocate their use so as to maximize a profit or service objective, or perhaps meet a demand while minimizing costs.

The following are some of the models used in scheduling and production control.

a. Linear programming model: Here all the constraints and objective functions are formulated as a linear equation and then problem is solved for optimality. Simplex method, transportation methods and assignment methods are major methods used here.

b. PERT/CPM network model: PERT/CPM network is the network showing the sequence of operations for a project and the precedence relation between the activities to be completed.

b) Note: Scheduling is done in all the activities of an organisation i.e., production, maintenance etc. Therefore, all the methods and techniques of scheduling is used for maintenance management (Ref. Chapter 8).

Escom-Coping with Runway Capacity Needs

ESCOM is a producer of electronic home appliances, including VHS (Video Home System) television recorders, located in northern California. The packaged product weighs about 75 kg. ESCOM was not the innovator of the system. Rather, its managers sat back and let RCA and others develop the market, and ESCOM is currently producing under license agreements. ESCOM has a conscious strategy of being a follower with new product innovations. It does not have the financial resources to be a leader in research and development.

ESCOM's present opportunity is indicated by the fact that industry sales of VHS recorders have increased 30 per cent per year for the past two years, and forecasts for the next year and the two following are even more enticing. ESCOM has established a 10 per cent market share position and feels that it can at least maintain this position if it has the needed capacity; it could possibly improve its market share if competitors fail to provide capacity at the time it is needed.

	Year					
	0	1	2	3	4	5
Forecast, 1000 Units	100	140	195	270	350	450
Capacity (gap), or slack 1000 units	5	(35)	(90)	(165)	(245)	(345)

The forecasts and capacity gaps are indicated in Table. ESCOM regards the first year forecast as being quite solid, based on its present market share and a compilation of several industry forecasts from different sources. It is less sure about the forecasts for future years, but it is basing these forecasts on patterns for both black and white and color TV sales during their product life cycles.

ESCOM's VHS model has a factory price of Rs 600. Variable costs are 70 percent of the price. Inventory carrying costs are 20 per cent of inventory value, 15 percentage points of which represents the cost of capital. ESCOM's facility planners estimate that a 40,000-unit plant can be built for Rs. 5 million and a 200,00-unit plant, for Rs. 10 million. Land and labour are available in the area, and either size plant can be built within a year.

(a) What capacity plans do you think ESCOM should make for next year? Why?

(b) What longer-term capacity plans should ESCOM make? Why?

(c) What are the implications of these plans for marketing, distribution, and production?

MULTIPLE CHOICE QUESTIONS

1. Product development is a central business activity because?
a) It is expensive and complicated
b) It determines organization's future
c) It is risky
d) All of the mentioned

Answer: d
Explanation: All of the conditions are reason for central activity.

2. Which of the following statement is false?
a) A product plan is a list of approved development projects, with strat and delivery dates
b) Marketing is a process of conceiving products and planning and executing their promotion, distribution, and exchange with customers
c) An opportunity funnel is a mechanism for collecting product ideas from specific source
d) None of the mentioned

Answer: c
Explanation: Opportunity funnel is a collection of ideas from diverse source.

3. Which of these is not a part of product planning?
a) Identification of opportunities
b) Evaluation and prioritizing opportunities
c) Allocation of resources and time determination
d) Finalizing process

Answer: d
Explanation: No such case is part of product planning.

4. How does marketers study customers and products for the generation of ideas?
a) Surveys
b) Focus Groups
c) Interviews
d) All of the mentioned

Answer: d
Explanation: All of these are part of idea generation.

5. Which of these does not account for Passive channels fo opportunity funnels?
a) Suggestion Lines
b) Bug-report Web pages
c) Monitoring trends
d) Awards for outstanding product ideas

Answer: c
Explanation: Monitoring trends are for active channels.

6. Which is not correct for an active channel?
a) Studying User to detect problems
b) Awards
c) Eliciting ideas through surveys, focus groups
d) Evaluating product strengths, needed features etc

Answer: b
Explanation: It follows the Passive channel.

7. Which of these is false about the opportunity statement?
a) Opportunity statement collects product ideas into opportunity funnel
b) Opportunity statement is brief description of product development idea
c) Opportunity statements for derivative and maintenance products summarize mass changes
d) None of the mentioned

Answer: a
Explanation: Product ideas are collected by opportunity funnel are stated in the opportunity statement and recorded database.

8. Decisions through which an organization follows development?
a) Competitive strategy
b) Accountability
c) All of the mentioned
d) None of the mentioned

Answer: a
Explanation: It is a procedure followed for development.

9. What are the factors Profitability depends on?
a) Eventual cost of product for development and marketing

b) Release of competitive product
c) Concern for target markets
d) All of the mentioned

Answer: d
Explanation: Targeted markets are concerned for profitability.

10. Which of these are incorrect for the product plan?
a) No need to revise product plan frequently
b) Product plan guides the launch of various product development activities
c) All of the mentioned
d) None of the mentioned

Answer: a
Explanation: Product plan is revised regularly.

11.Which of the following functions mentioned below of production planning and control are associated with the timetable of activities?
a) Scheduling
b) Dispatching
c) Expediting
d) Routing

Answer: a
Explanation
Scheduling is related to the timetable in production planning and control activities.

12. What among these takes a project mission statement as its input?
a) Generic Software Product Design
b) Generic Software Engineering Design
c) Generic Software Product & Engineering Design
d) None of the mentioned

Answer: a
Explanation: Software Product design input is project mission statement.

13. The design process where project mission statement is the input what will be its output?
a) Final design document
b) SRS

c) Product plan
d) Design document

Answer: b
Explanation: The design process is a generic software product design whose output is SRS.

14. Which of these are known as Project mission statement?
a) Business case document
b) Project charter
c) Project brief
d) All of the mentioned

Answer: d
Explanation: The project mission statement can be addressed by all of these.

15. What is the project mission statement?
a) It is a document that defines development project's goal
b) It is a document that specifies project's limits
c) It is a document that defines development project's goal & specifies project's limits
d) It is a document which specifies project mission

Answer: c
Explanation: The correct definition of project mission statement includes both.

16. The important roles followed by the project mission statement?
a) Launching a development project
b) Stating the software design problem
c) Both Launching a development project & Stating the software design problem
d) None of the mentioned

Answer: c
Explanation: The important roles include both activities.

17. Which of these is not a part of the project mission template?
a) Introduction
b) Product vision and project scope
c) Business requirements
d) Functional requirements

Answer: d
Explanation: It is a part of SRS and not project mission template.

18. Which of the following statement is correct?
a) Assumption is any factor that limits developers
b) Constraint is something that developers take it as granted
c) Constraint is a restriction on the solution
d) Assumption is drawback of the problem

Answer: c
Explanation: Rest all are false, Assumption is something that developers may take advantage for,
Constraint is any factor that limits developers,
Assumptions are feature of problem.

19. Which of these steps is not in sequence with project mission statement?
i. Introduction
ii. Target Markets
iii. Product vision and scope
iv. Business requirements
a) i and ii
b) ii and iii
c) ii and iv
d) iii and iv

Answer: b
Explanation: Product vision and scope is second step to be followed.

20. Which of these are true for product vision and project scope?
a) Product vision is general description of product's purpose and form
b) Project vision is work to be done in a project
c) Project scope is general description of product's purpose and form
d) None of the mentioned

Answer: a
Explanation: Only first definition is true rest all are incorrect.

21. Which among these is not a stakeholder?
a) Manager
b) Marketing person

c) User
d) Audience not a part of software who does not follow or has any concerns about software

Answer: d
Explanation: A stakeholder is anyone affected by product.

22. Which of the following statement is true?
a) The job of creating, modifying, and managing requirements over a product's lifetime is called requirement development
b) The portion of requirements engineering concerned with initially establishing requirements is termed requirements engineering
c) The portion of requirements engineering concerned with controlling requirements changes is called requirement management
d) All of the mentioned

Answer: c
Explanation: Rest all are false.

23. Which is true for SRS?
a) SRS is the main input of the software product design process
b) SRS is the main output to the engineering design process
c) SRS is also the main output of the requirements specification activity
d) All of the mentioned

Answer: c
Explanation: SRS is main output of the software product design process and vice versa.

24. SRS consists of?
a) Problem statement
b) Product design
c) Problem statement & Product design
d) None of the mentioned

Answer: c
Explanation: It includes both.

25. Which of these are non-technical requirements?
a) Functional Requirements
b) Non-Functional Requirements

c) Developer's Requirements
d) Data Requirements

Answer: c
Explanation: Developer's requirements are not necessary and also non technical one.

26. Which is true about functional requirements?
a) A functional requirement is also called behavioral requirement
b) A functional requirement includes development and operational requirements
c) A functional requirement is a statement of how a software product must map program inputs to program outputs
d) None of the mentioned

Answer: c
Explanation: Rest all options belongs to the non-functional requirements

27. Which of these are true for nonfunctional requirements?
a) A non-functional requirement is also called behavioral requirements
b) A non-functional requirement is a statement that a software product must have certain properties
c) It consists of Development and operational requirements
d) All of the mentioned

Answer: d
Explanation: Choices are true related to non-functional requirements.

28. Which of these does not belong to the qualities of development requirements?
a) Performance
b) Response time
c) Maintainability
d) Performance & Response time

Answer: d
Explanation: The other choices represents operational requirements

29. Which of these does not belong to the qualities of operational requirements?
a) Memory usage
b) Portability
c) Reusability

d) Portability & Reusability

Answer: d
Explanation: The choices represent development requirements

30. Which of the following does data requirements allow for data?
a) Entering data
b) Leaving data
c) Storing data in product
d) All of the mentioned

Answer: d
Explanation: All of these actions are followed by data requirements.

31. Technical level abstraction includes ______________
a) User level requirement
b) Physical level requirement
c) Operational level requirement
d) All of the mentioned

Answer: d
Explanation: All are the abstractions of technical requirements.

32. Which of the following statement is true?
a) A physical-level requirement is a statement about how a product must support stakeholders in achieving their goals or tasks
b) A operational-level requirement is a statement about the details of the physical form of a product, its physical interface to its environment, or its data formats
c) All of the mentioned
d) None of the mentioned

Answer: d
Explanation: Both of the choices represents incorrect definitions.

33. Which of the following statement is incorrect?
a) Interaction design, the activity of specifying products that people are able to – use effectively and enjoyably, is an essential part of product design and hence is part of requirements development
b) SRS templates structure product design documentation but must be adapted to the product's characteristics

c) Business requirements state client and development organization goals, while technical requirements state product details
d) None of the mentioned

Answer: d
Explanation: All of the choices are correct.

34. What does top down process follow?
a) The overall flow of activity during product design resolution is from higher to lower levels
b) The overall flow of activity during product design resolution is from lower to higher levels
c) All of the mentioned
d) None of the mentioned

Answer: a
Explanation: Top-down layer focuses on higher to lower abstraction.

35. What are the most common scenarios for resolutions?
a) Designers frequently work bottom up or skip levels of abstraction
b) To specify some part of product design to its physical level details before others are specified
c) All of the mentioned
d) None of the mentioned

Answer: c
Explanation: The choices represent the most common scenarios worked out under resolution techniques.

36. Lower level of abstraction includes?
a) Product features
b) Functions
c) Properties
d) All of the mentioned

Answer: d
Explanation: Lower abstraction includes all the choices mentioned.

37. Product design is mainly?
a) Top-down approach

b) Bottom-up approach
c) Top-down & Bottom-up approach
d) None of the mentioned

Answer: a
Explanation: Product design is top down approach.

38. The user-centered design comprises of which of these principles?
a) Stakeholder focus
b) Empirical Evaluation
c) Iteration
d) All of the mentioned

Answer: d
Explanation: It includes all the following principles.

39. Collection of stakeholder needs is called?
a) Requirements elicitation
b) Requirements validation
c) Needs Elicitation
d) Requirements & Needs elicitation

Answer: d
Explanation: Collection of stakeholders needs are called needs elicitation, needs identification, requirements elicitation.

40. Understanding Stakeholder needs are called?
a) Needs analysis
b) Needs elicitation
c) Needs identification
d) All of the mentioned

Answer: a
Explanation: Understanding of these needs are called needs analysis.

www.ingramcontent.com/pod-product-compliance
Ingram Content Group UK Ltd.
Pitfield, Milton Keynes, MK11 3LW, UK
UKHW061704190726
13853UKWH00008B/2398

9 789355 566195